The
Tony®
Award

THE ANTOINETTE PERRY AWARD

The medallion, which is three inches in diameter, is made of silver and depicts the masks of comedy and tragedy. The lucite stand measures approximately 3 3/4 by 3 3/4 inches.

The Tony® Award

A COMPLETE LISTING

*with a History of the
American Theatre Wing*

———— ☆ ————

Edited by
ISABELLE STEVENSON

HEINEMANN
Portsmouth, New Hampshire

Heinemann
A division of Reed Elsevier, Inc.
361 Hanover St.
Portsmouth, NH 03801-3912
Offices and agents throughout the world.

Library of Congress Cataloging-in-Publication Data
Stevenson, Isabelle, 1915–
    The Tony Award : a complete listing with a history of the American
Theatre Wing / edited by Isabelle Stevenson.
        p. cm.
    ISBN 0-435-08658-8 (alk. paper)
    Includes index.
    1. Tony awards. 2. American Theatre Wing. I. Title.
PN2270.A93S8 1994
792'.079'7471—dc20   94-36644
                                                          CIP

Editor: Lisa Barnett
Production: Melissa L. Inglis
Cover Design: Julie Hahn

Printed in the United States of America on acid-free paper.
99 98 97 96 95 94   EB   1 2 3 4 5 6 7 8 9

Contents

Preface

Since the inception of the Antoinette Perry Awards in 1947, the selection of categories and nominations by the committee has undergone many changes. The categories have, from season to season, been redefined, added to, and subtracted from, in order to remain flexible and to accommodate the individual and particular circumstances of each season.

The governing principle and yardstick for selecting a particular play, actor, etc., has, from the very beginning, been "distinguished achievement in the theatre" rather than "best." Therefore, there have been several occasions when the committee has selected two or three winners in the same category. For example, José Ferrer and Fredric March were both winners in the category of dramatic actor in 1947. Fiorello! and The Sound of Music both received Tonys in the musical category in 1960.

Until 1955, the selection of winners was announced, but the nominees were not. Therefore, during these first years there is no listing of nominations.

Certain categories were added over the years. For example, there was no Tony Award for lighting until 1970.

Since 1956 (with the exception of 1958), the American Theatre Wing's Tony nominations have been publicly announced in each category.

An asterisk denotes the winner in each category. The order of categories is not necessarily the order in which the Tonys were presented in a particular year.

The Special Awards presented each year were given for many

reasons: For example, Helen Menken's presentation to Gilbert Miller for his distinguished career as producer in the theatre; Cary Grant's tribute to Noel Coward for his contribution to the American theatre; and presentations to many others for their loyal and interested support of the theatre.

The Special Awards were presented to such shows as *Good Evening* and A *Thurber Carnival* for which there was no specific category but which merited recognition of their excellence.

The award was given posthumously to Helen Menken for her years of devoted service to the Wing as president and member of the board. Other special awards went to Rosamond Gilder, Vera Allen and Mrs. Martin Beck for their dedication and service. However, the Special Tony® is used sparingly and in recognition for a contribution to the theatre.

History of the American Theatre Wing

THE STAGE IS SET—THE CAST ASSEMBLES

If a Tony is ever given to the longest-running service organization in the theatre, it should go to the American Theatre Wing. The stage was set in 1917 when seven ladies—Rachel Crothers, Louise Closser Hale, Dorothy Donnelly, Josephine Hull, Minnie Dupree, Bessie Tryee, and Louise Drew—met to talk about the possibility of forming an organization to aid war relief. At that meeting it was decided to call members of the theatre world together for another meeting two weeks later. Word got around. The Hudson Theatre was packed. There were the internationally famous, together with wardrobe mistresses, stagehands, producers—people representing every segment of the family of "theatre." It took only two more weeks and the "Stage Women's War Relief" was functioning. Workrooms were immediately established for sewing—their output would eventually total 1,863,645 articles. Clothing and food collection centers were organized, a canteen for servicemen was set up on Broadway, and troops of entertainers were on their way to entertain wherever needed. Speakers were trained to sell Liberty Bonds—and they sold $10,000,000 worth of them. The "Stage Women's War Relief" was one of the most useful and active relief organizations in the world.

Even after the war their services continued. In 1920, at another mass meeting, the men formed their committee. This time, their efforts were on behalf of the civilian population still suffering from the effects of the war.

The need for relief activities diminished, but the organization continued. In 1939, Rachel Crothers was called upon to reactivate her committee. Josephine Hull and Minnie Dupree were members again, together with Antoinette Perry, Vera Allen, Gertrude Lawrence, Lucile Watson, Theresa Helburn, and Edith Atwater.

Many of the theatre's most distinguished performers worked far away from the footlights. One example was the workroom committee headed by Lucile Watson. Minutes from a June 9, 1940, meeting show that Peggy Conklin, Ruth Gordon, Uta Hagen, and Vivian Vance were a few of those serving in this capacity.

During this period, the organization was renamed the American Theatre Wing War Service, and was a branch of the British War Relief Society. Gilbert Miller, chairman of the men's division, staged a benefit to aid British air raid victims in 1941, and raised $40,000.

Directly after Pearl Harbor, the Wing became an independent organization. The forty-three who comprised the executive board and committee were a "Who's Who" of the theatre. Rachel Crothers was president; Gertrude Lawrence and Helen Hayes were first and second vice-presidents; Vera Allen, third vice-president; and Josephine Hull was treasurer. Antoinette Perry served as secretary.

The men's executive committee included Gilbert Miller, Brooks Atkinson, George S. Kaufman, Raymond Massey, Brock Pemberton, Billy Rose, Lee Shubert, Max Gordon, and Vinton Freedley; co-chairwomen were Jane Cowl and Selena Royle.

The Hudson Theatre was again the scene for a mass meeting of the entertainment industry, and from this came some of the Wing's most famous activities. Perhaps the most famous were the Stage Door Canteens. There were eight in cities around the country, as well as in London and Paris. Alfred Lunt was the food expert, Katharine Cornell helped in the kitchen, Marlene Dietrich was frequently on hand at the milk bar, and Dorothy Fields did "KP." Alan Hewitt was co-chairman; Radie Harris, chairman of the entertainment committee, brought in the talent to work at the Canteen; and Jean Dalrymple, who was Rachel Crothers' first publicity volunteer, became the chairman of the publicity committee. Speakers, trained by the Wing, sold bonds. With the money raised from the movie *Stage Door Canteen*, the Wing was able to give $75,000 to the USO to inaugurate legitimate drama as entertainment for soldiers overseas. The first play was *The Barretts of Wimpole Street*, starring Katharine Cornell. The weekly radio program "Stage Door Canteen" was another source of income. The "Lunchtime Follies" went out to entertain factory workers. Lunch was sometimes at midnight.

As a sample of the Wing's activities—and accomplishments—in New York, during the war and the first eight months after, the Wing sent out nearly 1,500 auditorium programs, 350 legitimate plays, and over 6,700 ward units, using, in all, well over 40,000 volunteers.

At the Wing's peak there were twenty-five hospitals within a radius of seventy-five miles of New York. The Wing was sending out about one thousand, two hundred entertainers each month. During that same period, flying with the Naval Air Corps, the Wing sent units to ten Naval and Marine hospitals. In all, ninety-seven units, including plays, using 617 people, were flown for weekend hospital performances for the Navy.

The monthly aggregate during the first postwar year was still 650 people a month. Branches of the Wing in Washington, D.C., and Boston had equally impressive records.

In the spring of 1947 the Wing took another dramatic step. A specialized recreation program was begun, and the teaching of its technique to staff and volunteer workers in each of the neuro-psychiatric hospitals under the Veterans Administration was started. Teams of Wing actresses, selected for their experience and particular qualities, resigned their theatre and radio jobs for a three-and-a-half-month tour.

Vera Allen, Ben Grauer, Elaine Perry, and Russel Crouse are but a few who were active on the hospital committee.

For those families beginning to face the homecoming of wounded and the problems brought on by separation, the Wing created the Community Players. Outstanding playwrights wrote short plays dramatizing specific problems, which served as catalysts for family discussion.

Katharine Cornell and Mrs. Henry N. Pratt were co-chairwomen. Vera Allen, Mrs. Paul Raymer, and Cornelia Otis Skinner served as vice-chairwomen.

At the peak of the war there were fifty-four separate Wing activities, any one of which would have ranked as a major war service.

When the war was finally over, the Wing turned its attention to the returning veteran. On September 13, 1945, a letter went to all members calling for the first meeting of the planning committee for postwar activities. The committee met the following week.

One of the plans put into motion was to have a theatre school for the returning veterans. On July 8, 1946, the American Theatre Wing Professional Training School opened its doors. The founders of the school were Vera Allen, Mary Hunter, and Winston O'Keefe, who also served as the school director. Theresa Helburn, Maurice Evans, and Louis Simon were among those on the advisory committee. Mr. Simon succeeded Mr. O'Keefe as director.

School hours were 10 AM to midnight, and the students were from all areas of theatre, representing every theatre union. The original curriculum grew from twenty-three to fifty courses offered.

To name all those who taught would be to list almost every distinguished name from theatre, television, the opera, and music. Leon Barzin and Joseph Rosenstock taught conducting. Alfred Lunt, Lehman Engell, Eva Le Gallienne, Sir Cedric Hardwicke, Cyril Ritchard, Jose Ferrer, and Maureen Stapleton taught acting. Martha Graham, Hanya Holm, Jose Limon, Charles Weidman, Ray Bolger, and Katherine Dunham taught dance. Kermit Bloomgarden lectured on producing and brought in fellow producers as guests. Delbert Mann and Ezra Stone headed TV workshops.

There were courses in Hebrew liturgical singing and repertoire, management problems, and one on music for actors and directors taught by Richard Rodgers and Oscar Hammerstein II.

Among Wing students, all professionals, but not yet famous, were Russell Nype, Pat Hingle, Tony Randall, William Warfield, Charlton Heston, Gordon Macrae, and James Whitmore, as well as leading singers of the Met and the New York City Opera Company who came to improve their acting.

Marge and Gower Champion, already a starring dance team, came to study music. At its peak, one thousand, two hundred were enrolled in the school, many of them studying on their GI Bill of Rights. The school continued to fulfill its obligation to veterans for well over a decade.

Today the American Theatre Wing continues its programs to further the highest standards of the theatre. Rachel Crothers held her first meeting in 1917 and thirty years later the first Tony® Awards were given. That original idea of professional service to the community and high quality of performance continues in the Wing's present activities.

The Wing is concerned with youth—with seeing that the theatre is brought to young people in as many community areas as possible. This is done via its support of "Saturday Theatre for Children," which brings quality live theatre to the school auditoriums. These public schools, in the five boroughs, are, for the most part, in low-income neighborhoods. As a Rockefeller Foundation study showed, the great majority of those who attend the theatre regularly today are those who attended the theatre regularly as children. The Wing is concerned with educating and building the audience that will support tomorrow's theatre. Another program, "Introduction to Broadway," enables junior and senior high school students to attend Broadway shows. Through the cooperation of the producers, the New York City Board of Education, and the American Theatre

Wing, a minimal ticket price is established. The student pays half and the Wing pays half. As part of the program, students meet with cast members after the show. The Wing is an organization through which the theatre can give direct service to the community.

In the tradition of its hospital program during two world wars, the Wing continues to bring professional productions from Broadway and Off-Off Broadway to veteran's hospitals, institutions, and AIDS centers.

The Wing also sponsors seminars on "Working in the Theatre." These are held in the spring and fall of each year for students and professional members of the various theatrical unions. Here, they have the opportunity to listen and talk to some of America's most distinguished actors, directors, producers, and playwrights. These seminars are moderated by Wing Board Members Jean Dalrymple, Brendan Gill, and Henry Hewes, as well as Schuyler Chapin, George C. White and Edwin Wilson, among others; and are chaired by the Wing's president, Isabelle Stevenson. Tony® Award winners such as Jane Alexander, Michael Bennett, Matthew Broderick, Len Cariou, Glenn Close, Alexander Cohen, Larry Fishburne, Bob Fosse, Charles Fuller, Morton Gottlieb, Gregory Hines, Angela Lansbury, Michael Moriarty, Joseph Papp, Harold Prince, Peter Shaffer, Carole Shelley, Stephen Sondheim, Michael Stewart, Jessica Tandy, Tommy Tune, Robin Wagner, Lanford Wilson, and Patricia Zipprodt have been just a few of those who have given freely of their time for this valuable program. The audience also participates in a question-and-answer period with the panelists at the end of each seminar. These programs have been videotaped by the City University of New York's educational cable television station and are broadcast over CUNY-TV.

In 1982, the American Theatre Wing established the Clarence Ross Fellowship Master Class Program for professional actors, in collaboration with the O'Neill Theater Center. The Fellows studied with Rudi Shelley of the Bristol Old Vic and Lynn Britt, director of the O'Neill's Theater Institute.

Private contributions, fund-raising efforts, membership dues, and a portion of the proceeds from the Tony® Award telecasts support all of the Wing's programs.

The Wing's activities continue to expand under the direction of Mrs. John Stevenson, who has been a board member since 1957 and succeeded Helen Menken as president in 1966.

In recent years the Wing's scholarship programs have been enlarged. Recognizing the importance of and need for new playwrights, grants are made to the Eugene O'Neill Theater Center, The New Dramatists, Playwrights Horizons, and to developing theatre companies. The American Theatre Wing's annual scholarships are also awarded to the American Academy of Dramatic Arts. The Wing was a sponsor of FACT, the First American Congress of Theatre, held in Princeton, New Jersey, in 1974.

Isabelle Stevenson, like her predecessors, had been actively engaged in the theatre and, prior to her marriage, appeared in theatres throughout the country, Europe, and Australia. She is active in theatre and community-oriented programs.

Board of Directors

Richard Brandt
Donald Brooks
Jan Chipman
Jean Dalrymple
Dasha Epstein
Brendan Gill
Mrs. Ruth Goddard
William Hammerstein
Jay S. Harris
Radie Harris
Marlene Hess
Henry Hewes
Douglas Leeds
Jo Sullivan Loesser
Michael Price
Lloyd Richards
John Stevenson
Mrs. John Stevenson
Mrs. Donald Stralem
Tommy Valando
Richard Weaver
Rose Wohlstetter

Board of Advisors

Glenn Close
Patricia Crown
Lawrence P. Fraiberg
David Geffen
Jack Hausman
Shirley Herz
Jonathan Herzog
Cornelius F. Keating
Ellen Krass
Ann Loring
Lucille Lortel
David Merrick
Ward Morehouse III
Leo Nevas
Ann Reinking
Howard Richmond
Jean Stapleton
Dorothy Strelsin
Robert Whitehead
Arthur Whitelaw

Past Presidents and Chairwomen

Rachel Crothers
Antoinette Perry
Helen Hayes
Vera Allen
Mrs. Martin Beck
Helen Menken

The Antoinette Perry (Tony®) Awards

ANTOINETTE PERRY
(1888–1946)

Actress, producer, director, chairman of the board, and secretary of the American Theatre Wing. The Tony® Awards were named in her honor.

The Tony®, named in honor of Antoinette Perry, has been one of the theatre's most coveted awards and is annually bestowed on professionals for "distinguished achievement" in the theatre and not for the "best" in any category.

When Antoinette Perry died in 1946 at the age of fifty-eight, many people who knew her were determined that she would not be forgotten. As chairman of the board and secretary of the American Theatre Wing throughout World War II, Antoinette Perry insisted on perfection and high standards of quality. Her dedication and tireless efforts to broaden the scope of theatre through the many programs of the American Theatre Wing affected hundreds of people.

Antoinette Perry made her first impact on the theatre in 1906, when she was only eighteen. She played opposite David Warfield in *Music Master* and, the following year, in David Belasco's A *Grand Army Man*. Only two years later, and at an age when most actresses are still waiting for that first big break, Antoinette Perry retired, a star, to marry and raise a family.

Her daughters, Elaine and Margaret, pursued acting careers in the theatre. Elaine became an active member of the American Theatre Wing as well, and Margaret, who understudied Ingrid Bergman in *Liliom*, stage-managed the touring production of *The Barretts of Wimpole Street*.

In 1922, after the death of her husband, Antoinette Perry returned to the stage and appeared in many plays, including *Minick*, by George S. Kaufman and Edna Ferber, in 1924, and Margaret Anglin's 1927 production of *Electra*. In association with Brock Pemberton, she then turned her talent to directing, enriching the theatre with several memorable plays, including Preston Sturges' comedy *Strictly Dishonorable*, in 1929 and Mary Chase's classic, *Harvey*, in 1944.

When Antoinette Perry died, it was Jacob Wilk who first suggested the idea of an Antoinette Perry Memorial to John Golden. He, in turn, presented the idea to the Wing. Brock Pemberton, a long-time personal friend as well as business associate, was appointed chairman of the committee, and suggested that the Wing give a series of annual awards in her name. A panel of six members was appointed to nominate candidates for the award in each category. The members who made the final selections in the first year were: Vera Allen, Louise Beck, Jane Cowl, Helen Hayes, Brooks Atkinson, Kermit Bloomgarden, Clayton Collyer, George Heller, Rudy Karnolt, Burns Mantle, Gilbert Miller, Warren P. Munsell, Solly Pernick, James E. Sauter, and Oliver Sayler.

The first awards were made at a dinner in the Grand Ballroom of the Waldorf Astoria on Easter Sunday, April 6, 1947. With Vera Allen, Antoinette Perry's successor as Wing chairwoman, presiding, the evening included dining, dancing, and a program of entertainment whose participants included Mickey Rooney, Herb Shriner, Ethel Waters, and David Wayne.

The following year, Mrs. Martin Beck, one of the Wing's founders, succeeded Vera Allen as chairwoman of the board. When Mrs. Beck retired, the distinguished actress Helen Menken presided in that office until 1957 when she became president of the Wing. She succeeded Helen Hayes, who was elected in 1950. Until her death in 1966, Helen Menken devoted herself to the

Wing and its numerous programs, including the yearly presentation of the Tony® Awards. Mrs. John Stevenson, an active board member for seventeen years, was elected president and remains so today.

During the first two years, there was no official Tony® award. The winners were presented with, in addition to a scroll, a cigarette lighter or a compact. The United Scenic Artists sponsored a contest for a suitable design for the award and Herman Rosse's entry, depicting the masks of comedy and tragedy on one side and the profile of Antoinette Perry on the other, was selected. In 1949, the medallion was initiated at the third annual dinner. It continues to be the official Tony® Award.

From 1947 until 1965, the dinner and Tony® Award presentation were held in various ballrooms of such hotels as the Plaza, the Waldorf Astoria, and the Hotel Astor. The ceremonies were broadcast over WOR radio and The Mutual Network and, in 1956, televised for the first time on Du Mont's Channel 5. Brock Pemberton, Mrs. Martin Beck, Helen Hayes, and Ilka Chase presided over the ceremonies and award presentations and entertainment was provided by such notables of the theatre as Katherine Cornell, Guthrie McClintic, Helen Hayes, Ralph Bellamy, Joan Crawford, Alfred de Liagre Jr., Gilbert Miller, Shirley Booth, Carol Channing, Joan Fontaine, Paul Newman, Geraldine Page, Anne Bancroft, Sidney Poitier, Fredric March, Robert Goulet, Gig Young, Anna Maria Alberghetti, Henry Fonda, Patricia Neal, and many others.

In spite of the death of Helen Menken in March of 1966, the awards were presented at the Rainbow Room the following month. The ceremony was subdued and, for the first and only time, held in the afternoon without public attendance or entertainment. Both factors have, since the inception of the awards up to the present day Tony® ceremony, been important to the program.

Considered a vital influence in the theatre, representing quality and distinction, the League of New York Theatres— renamed the League of American Theatres and Producers, Inc.— was authorized by the American Theatre Wing to present the Tony® Awards in 1967 when the ceremonies were moved from the traditional hotel ballroom setting to a Broadway theatre at the suggestion of Alvin Cooperman, who was vice president of special programs at NBC–TV. Alexander H. Cohen produced the nationwide television show and organized the ball and supper dance after the awards. The American Theatre Wing continues to preserve the original quality of intimacy by holding a party each year at Sardi's for Wing members and friends that salutes the Tony® and the Stage Door Canteen.

In 1971, Alexander H. Cohen, producer of the American Theatre Wing's Tony® show, marked the twenty-fifth anniversary of the Antoinette Perry Awards. In celebration of such an auspicious event, the entertainment for that year was an extraordinary, show-stopping recapitulation of the past. David Wayne, Nanette Fabray, Alfred Drake, Ray Walston, Vivian Blaine, Sam Levene, Yul Brynner, Patricia Morrison (subbing for the late Gertrude Lawrence), Edie Adams, Gwen Verdon, John Raitt, Stanley Holloway, Robert Preston, Richard Kiley, Tom Bosley, Florence Henderson (subbing for Mary Martin), Paul Lynde, Zero Mostel, Carol Channing, Angela Lansbury, Jill Hayworth, Leslie Uggams, William Daniels, Virginia Vestoff, and Lauren Bacall magically and magnificently recreated musical moments of the roles for which they had been awarded the Tony® in past seasons.

VOTING

In 1947, the originating committee devised a voting system whose eligible voters were members of the board of the American Theatre Wing, representing management, and the performer and craft unions of the entertainment field. In 1954, voting eligibility was expanded to include theatre professionals who were not members of the American Theatre Wing. Today the system has been further enlarged. Persons eligible to vote for winners of the Tony® Awards, besides the board of directors of the American Theatre Wing, are members of the governing boards of Actors' Equity Association, the Dramatists Guild, the Society of Stage Directors and Choreographers, the United Scenic Artists, those persons whose names appear on the first and second night press lists, and the membership of the League of American Theatres and Producers, an approximate total of 650.

Throughout the long, distinguished history of the Tony® Awards, selections of nominees and winners have been executed with the principle of awarding for excellence and distinguished achievement. Although the presentations have gone through many changes, the basic principles and standards remain constant.

Reflections from 1994 Tony® Award Winners

The extraordinary thing about the Tonys® is that all of New York City takes part in this celebration of theatre. If you've been lucky enough to be nominated, congratulations come thick and fast in the intervening weeks before the ceremony. From shop assistants, waiters, restauranteurs, lavatory attendants, the boys from the fire station on Eighth Avenue, even total strangers in the street murmur "Good Luck" as they pass.

I had been nominated twice before, but some fifteen years ago, and my memory of the ceremonies are pretty hazy. However, I do remember the first occasion, arriving at the theatre at the same time as Maggie Smith and Elizabeth Ashley. We were all up for best actress, and we were all dressed in black. As we made our way up the stairs, I heard Maggie remark, "When shall we three meet again?" Maureen Stapleton won the award that day, I think.

This time, as on all previous times, I arrived with little anticipation of winning. I had a speech, of sorts, but it was pitifully unprepared—and then I heard my name. Suprised, joy and dread of making a hash of my speech followed, and I mounted the stairs to accept.

The award now sits on my mantlepiece at home, as a tangible reminder of a wonderfully happy run on Broadway.

As I write, New York prepares for a new season. Off with the old, on with the new—that is as it should be.

Diana Rigg
Actress (Play), *Medea*

I am very fortunate that the role of Fosca came into my life at a time when I was prepared to give it the kind of commitment, discipline, energy, sense of abandon, and compassion that she demanded from an actress. I had dreamed of working on a Sondheim-Lapine show since seeing *Sunday in The Park With George*—and being inspired beyond words. To be able to channel my work into a piece that dares to be difficult, that challenges and provokes me and our audiences—I thank God every day.

And to be honored by my colleagues and the American Theatre Wing with the Tony®, that is, quite frankly, still a bit unreal to me. I am proud, excited, exhausted, and thrilled to be a part of a "tradition" that I've enjoyed as a celebration of theater for many years.

Donna Murphy
Actress (Musical), *Passion*

I really only remember spurts of the evening: putting on my dress during the two commercial breaks and rushing to my seat panicked because I couldn't find my lucky origami star. I wasn't hungry and hadn't eaten in about a week. So when I was finally standing at the podium after what seemed an endless "I-hope-I-don't-trip" walk to the stage, I had just two thoughts: "What am I going to say?" and "I really want a quarter pounder with cheese!"

Audra Ann McDonald
Actress (Featured Role—Musical), *Carousel*

At the heart of *Carousel* are "a couple of specks of Nothing": two little people—Billy and Julie—who find a desperate refuge in each other against a hostile world and their own poor opinions of themselves. It's a show about loneliness.

It's also a show about the urgent need to believe that you need never walk alone. Julie is urged to believe it as she weeps over Billy's stiffening corpse; and the whole community joins hands to reaffirm their belief as Billy's daughter makes her first tentative step towards them.

Like all great plays, and like Life, *Carousel* is as ambiguous as it is deeply felt. The doomed pair at its centre are as alone and dislocated as the horny kids who dance "June" together are at ease with themselves. Love heals, and love destroys. Hope jostles with despair, and both can pierce the heart.

Rodgers and Hammerstein took Billy and Julie, and their lonely confusion, from their European source—Ferenc Molnar's *Liliom*. The energy and hope offered by the mill-town community of which they are part are Rodgers and Hammerstein's invention; and for me—a European directing an American masterpiece on Broadway—they seemed to be profoundly American inventions, and entirely born out of my experience working here. I have never enjoyed anything more.

It was the Rodgers and Hammerstein families who let me loose; being themselves distinguished and adventurous theatre people, they were unwavering in their support of the idea of a new look at their fathers' brilliant show. My colleagues at the National Theatre in London nurtured the production. And my friends at Lincoln Center have given me the time of my life. To have won the Tony® Award for it seems greater good fortune than anyone deserves.

Nicholas Hytner
Director (Musical), *Carousel*

The Tony® Award is something I have spent half my life dreaming of achieving and striving to be worthy of. Now, upon reflection, I know no one person wins a Tony®. A team of collaborative artists gives birth to an idea and carries it with devotion through its childhood and into its adulthood.

To me, the Tony® is my director calling at midnight with a new idea, it's my wonderful actors figuring out how to use a costume to best advantage, or it's my cherished drapers taking me aside to look at a new way to put two trims together for a better effect on a costume.

My Tony® belongs more to these loving and brilliantly talented people than to me. I am so lucky to have them!

Ann Hould-Ward
Costume Designer, *Beauty and the Beast*

The best theatre is a seamless collaboration between direction, performance, design, and technical production. An *Inspector Calls* uses an extraordinary environment to reveal a familliar play's passion. The lighting aims to help the audience "inspect" the characters by giving them a special intensity in a foreboding setting. All the other aspects of the production compliment this approach.

I am grateful for this terrific teamwork. I also cannot help think back to summer stock in Philadelphia, fringe theatre in

London, and the encouragement of so many people on the 20 year road to this Broadway production. Having watched the Tonys® as a stage struck child, I never dreamed I would have the honor to take one home.

Rick Fisher
Lighting Designer, *An Inspector Calls*

Categories of Awards

Best Play—*Award to Author; Award to Producer*
Best Musical—*Award to Producer*
Best Book of a Musical
Best Original Score (*Music and Lyrics*) Written for the Theatre
Best Performance by a Leading Actor in a Play
Best Performance by a Leading Actress in a Play
Best Performance by a Leading Actor in a Musical
Best Performance by a Leading Actress in a Musical
Best Performance by a Featured Actor in a Play
Best Performance by a Featured Actress in a Play
Best Performance by a Featured Actor in a Musical
Best Performance by a Featured Actress in a Musical
Best Direction of a Play
Best Direction of a Musical
Best Scenic Design
Best Costume Design
Best Lighting Design
Best Choreography
Best Revival—Play or Musical
Special Awards

The 1940s

"In 1948, the second year that the Tony® Awards were presented, I had a non-speaking part in Robinson Jeffers' 'Medea,' and Judith Anderson won a Tony® for her brilliant performance. It was the first play I had been in on Broadway. I do not remember dreaming of such an award.

Nineteen years later I received a nomination for my performance as Julia in Edward Albee's 'A Delicate Balance' (and won) and four years after that, for a leading performance in Oliver Hailey's 'Father's Day' (and did not win).

Looking back, it was the nomination that meant the most to me both times. I admired the actresses in my categories and was proud to be listed with them.

The thrill of winning lasts a minute. The memory of rehearsing, playing the parts, sharing them with audiences lasts much longer. And in some special way the recognition of the Tony® committee makes the memories seem even dearer.

Each time I felt that the part won—the playwright won—and I accepted the Award and the scroll for them. So I treasure both and always will."

Marian Seldes

1947

ACTORS (DRAMATIC)
☆ José Ferrer, *Cyrano de Bergerac*
☆ Fredric March, *Years Ago*

ACTRESSES (DRAMATIC)
☆ Ingrid Bergman, *Joan of Lorraine*
☆ Helen Hayes, *Happy Birthday*

ACTRESS, SUPPORTING OR FEATURED (DRAMATIC)
☆ Patricia Neal, *Another Part of the Forest*

ACTOR, SUPPORTING OR FEATURED (MUSICAL)
☆ David Wayne, *Finian's Rainbow*

DIRECTOR
☆ Elia Kazan, *All My Sons*

COSTUMES
☆ Lucinda Ballard, *Happy Birthday* / *Another Part of the Forest* / *Street Scene* / *John Loves Mary* / *The Chocolate Soldier*
David Ffolkes, *Henry VIII*

CHOREOGRAPHERS
☆ Agnes de Mille, *Brigadoon*
☆ Michael Kidd, *Finian's Rainbow*

SPECIAL AWARDS
☆ Dora Chamberlain
☆ Mr. and Mrs. Ira Katzenberg
☆ Jules Leventhal
☆ Burns Mantle
☆ P. A. MacDonald
☆ Arthur Miller
☆ Vincent Sardi, Sr.
☆ Kurt Weill

1948

ACTORS (DRAMATIC)
☆ Henry Fonda, *Mister Roberts*
☆ Paul Kelly, *Command Decision*
☆ Basil Rathbone, *The Heiress*

ACTRESSES (DRAMATIC)
☆ Judith Anderson, *Medea*
☆ Katharine Cornell, *Antony and Cleopatra*
☆ Jessica Tandy, *A Streetcar Named Desire*

ACTOR (MUSICAL)
☆ Paul Hartman, *Angel in the Wings*

ACTRESS (MUSICAL)
☆ Grace Hartman, *Angel in the Wings*

PLAY
☆ *Mister Roberts* by Thomas Heggen and Joshua Logan/based on the Thomas Heggen novel.

PRODUCER
☆ Leland Hayward, *Mister Roberts*

AUTHORS
☆ Thomas Heggen and Joshua Logan, *Mister Roberts*

COSTUMES
☆ Mary Percy Schenck, *The Heiress*

SCENIC DESIGNER
☆ Horace Armistead, *The Medium*

CHOREOGRAPHER
☆ Jerome Robbins, *High Button Shoes*

STAGE TECHNICIANS
☆ George Gebhardt
☆ George Pierce

SPECIAL AWARDS
☆ Vera Allen
☆ Paul Beisman
☆ Joe E. Brown
☆ Robert Dowling
☆ Experimental Theatre, Inc.
☆ Rosamond Gilder
☆ June Lockhart
☆ Mary Martin
☆ Robert Porterfield
☆ James Whitmore

1949

ACTOR (DRAMATIC)
☆ Rex Harrison, *Anne of the Thousand Days*

ACTRESS (DRAMATIC)
☆ Martita Hunt, *The Madwoman of Chaillot*

ACTOR, SUPPORTING OR FEATURED (DRAMATIC)
☆ Arthur Kennedy, *Death of a Salesman*

ACTRESS, SUPPORTING OR FEATURED (DRAMATIC)
☆ Shirley Booth, *Goodbye, My Fancy*

ACTOR (MUSICAL)
☆ Ray Bolger, *Where's Charley?*

ACTRESS (MUSICAL)
☆ Nanette Fabray, *Love Life*

PLAY
☆ *Death of a Salesman* by Arthur Miller

PRODUCERS (DRAMATIC)
☆ Kermit Bloomgarden and Walter Fried, *Death of a Salesman*

AUTHOR
☆ Arthur Miller, *Death of a Salesman*

DIRECTOR
☆ Elia Kazan, *Death of a Salesman*

MUSICAL
☆ *Kiss Me Kate*. Music and lyrics by Cole Porter, book by Bella and Samuel Spewack

PRODUCERS (MUSICAL)
☆ Saint-Subber and Lemuel Ayers, *Kiss Me Kate*

AUTHORS (MUSICAL)
☆ Bella and Samuel Spewack, *Kiss Me Kate*

COMPOSER AND LYRICIST
☆ Cole Porter, *Kiss Me Kate*

COSTUMES
☆ Lemuel Ayers, *Kiss Me Kate*

SCENIC DESIGNER
☆ Jo Mielziner, *Sleepy Hollow / Summer and Smoke / Anne of the Thousand Days / Death of a Salesman / South Pacific*

CHOREOGRAPHER
☆ Gower Champion, *Lend An Ear*

CONDUCTOR AND MUSICAL DIRECTOR
☆ Max Meth, *As the Girls Go*

The 1950s

"There are two types of people. One type asserts that awards mean nothing to them. The second type breaks out into tears upon receiving an award, and thanks their mother, father, children, the producer, the director—and, if they can crowd it in—the American Baseball League.

However, I believe that people in the theatre who receive this award have a special feeling that makes them cherish the winning of a Tony. It prevents them from going on effusively. The Tony has a special value. It was created to award distinguished achievement in the theatre."

Dore Schary

1950

ACTOR (DRAMATIC)
☆ Sidney Blackmer, *Come Back, Little Sheba*

ACTRESS (DRAMATIC)
☆ Shirley Booth, *Come Back, Little Sheba*

ACTOR (MUSICAL)
☆ Ezio Pinza, *South Pacific*

ACTRESS (MUSICAL)
☆ Mary Martin, *South Pacific*

ACTOR, SUPPORTING OR FEATURED (MUSICAL)
☆ Myron McCormick, *South Pacific*

ACTRESS, SUPPORTING OR FEATURED (MUSICAL)
☆ Juanita Hall, *South Pacific*

PLAY
☆ *The Cocktail Party* by T. S. Eliot

PRODUCER (DRAMATIC)
☆ Gilbert Miller, *The Cocktail Party*

AUTHOR (DRAMATIC)
☆ T. S. Eliot, *The Cocktail Party*

DIRECTOR
☆ Joshua Logan, *South Pacific*

MUSICAL
☆ *South Pacific.* Music by Richard Rodgers, lyrics by Oscar Hammerstein II, book by Oscar Hammerstein II and Joshua Logan

PRODUCERS (MUSICAL)
☆ Richard Rodgers, Oscar Hammerstein II, Leland Hayward, and Joshua Logan, *South Pacific*

AUTHORS (MUSICAL)
☆ Oscar Hammerstein II and Joshua Logan, *South Pacific*

COMPOSER
☆ Richard Rodgers, *South Pacific*

COSTUMES
☆ Aline Bernstein, *Regina*

SCENIC DESIGNER
☆ Jo Mielziner, *The Innocents*

CHOREOGRAPHER
☆ Helen Tamiris, *Touch and Go*

CONDUCTOR AND MUSICAL DIRECTOR
☆ Maurice Abravanel, *Regina*

STAGE TECHNICIAN
☆ Joe Lynn, master propertyman, *Miss Liberty*

SPECIAL AWARDS
☆ Maurice Evans
☆ Mrs. Eleanor Roosevelt presented a special award to a volunteer worker of the American Theatre Wing's hospital program.

1951

ACTOR (DRAMATIC)
☆ Claude Rains, *Darkness At Noon*

ACTRESS (DRAMATIC)
☆ Uta Hagen, *The Country Girl*

ACTOR, SUPPORTING OR FEATURED (DRAMATIC)
☆ Eli Wallach, *The Rose Tattoo*

ACTRESS, SUPPORTING OR FEATURED (DRAMATIC)
☆ Maureen Stapleton, *The Rose Tattoo*

ACTOR (MUSICAL)
☆ Robert Alda, *Guys and Dolls*

ACTRESS (MUSICAL)
☆ Ethel Merman, *Call Me Madam*

ACTOR, SUPPORTING OR FEATURED (MUSICAL)
☆ Russell Nype, *Call Me Madam*

ACTRESS, SUPPORTING OR FEATURED (MUSICAL)
☆ Isabel Bigley, *Guys and Dolls*

PLAY
☆ *The Rose Tattoo* by Tennesee Williams

PRODUCER (DRAMATIC)
☆ Cheryl Crawford, *The Rose Tattoo*

AUTHOR (DRAMATIC)
☆ Tennessee Williams, *The Rose Tattoo*

DIRECTOR
☆ George S. Kaufman, *Guys and Dolls*

MUSICAL
☆ *Guys and Dolls*. Music and lyrics by Frank Loesser, book by Jo
   Swerling and Abe Burrows

PRODUCERS (MUSICAL)
☆ Cy Feuer and Ernest H. Martin, *Guys and Dolls*

AUTHORS (MUSICAL)
☆ Jo Swerling and Abe Burrows, *Guys and Dolls*

COMPOSER AND LYRICIST
☆ Frank Loesser, *Guys and Dolls*

COSTUMES
☆ Miles White, *Bless You All*

SCENIC DESIGNER
☆ Boris Aronson, *The Rose Tattoo* / *The Country Girl* / *Season In The Sun*

CHOREOGRAPHER
☆ Michael Kidd, *Guys and Dolls*

CONDUCTER AND MUSICAL DIRECTOR
☆ Lehman Engel, *The Consul*

STAGE TECHNICIAN
☆ Richard Raven, *The Autumn Garden*

SPECIAL AWARD
☆ Ruth Green

1952

ACTOR (DRAMATIC)
☆ José Ferrer, *The Shrike*

ACTRESS (DRAMATIC)
☆ Julie Harris, *I Am a Camera*

ACTRESS (MUSICAL)
☆ Gertrude Lawrence, *The King & I*

ACTOR (MUSICAL)
☆ Phil Silvers, *Top Banana*

ACTOR, SUPPORTING OR FEATURED (DRAMATIC)
☆ John Cromwell, *Point of No Return*

ACTRESS, SUPPORTING OR FEATURED (DRAMATIC)
☆ Marian Winters, *I Am a Camera*

ACTOR, SUPPORTING OR FEATURED (MUSICAL)
☆ Yul Brynner, *The King & I*

ACTRESS, SUPPORTING OR FEATURED (MUSICAL)
☆ Helen Gallagher, *Pal Joey*

PLAY
☆ *The Fourposter* by Jan de Hartog

MUSICAL
☆ *The King & I.* Book and lyrics by Oscar Hammerstein II, music
   by Richard Rodgers

DIRECTOR
☆ José Ferrer, *The Shrike / The Fourposter / Stalag* 17

COSTUMES
☆ Irene Sharaff, *The King & I*

SCENIC DESIGNER
☆ Jo Mielziner, *The King & I*

CHOREOGRAPHER
☆ Robert Alton, *Pal Joey*

CONDUCTOR AND MUSICAL DIRECTOR
☆ Max Meth, *Pal Joey*

STAGE TECHNICIAN
☆ Peter Feller, master carpenter for *Call Me Madam*

SPECIAL AWARDS
☆ Edward Kook
☆ Judy Garland
☆ Charles Boyer

1953

ACTOR (DRAMATIC)
☆ Tom Ewell, *The Seven Year Itch*

ACTRESS (DRAMATIC)
☆ Shirley Booth, *Time of the Cuckoo*

ACTOR, SUPPORTING OR FEATURED (DRAMATIC)
☆ John Williams, *Dial M for Murder*

ACTRESS, SUPPORTING OR FEATURED (DRAMATIC)
☆ Beatrice Straight, *The Crucible*

ACTOR (MUSICAL)
☆ Thomas Mitchell, *Hazel Flagg*

ACTRESS (MUSICAL)
☆ Rosalind Russell, *Wonderful Town*

ACTOR, SUPPORTING OR FEATURED (MUSICAL)
☆ Hiram Sherman, *Two's Company*

ACTRESS, SUPPORTING OR FEATURED (MUSICAL)
☆ Sheila Bond, *Wish You Were Here*

PLAY
☆ *The Crucible* by Arthur Miller

PRODUCER (DRAMATIC)
☆ Kermit Bloomgarden, *The Crucible*

AUTHOR (DRAMATIC)
☆ Arthur Miller, *The Crucible*

DIRECTOR
☆ Joshua Logan, *Picnic*

MUSICAL
☆ *Wonderful Town.* Book by Joseph Fields and Jerome Chodorov, music by Leonard Bernstein, lyrics by Betty Comden and Adolph Green

PRODUCER (MUSICAL)
☆ Robert Fryer, *Wonderful Town*

AUTHORS (MUSICAL)
☆ Joseph Fields and Jerome Chodorov, *Wonderful Town*

COMPOSER
☆ Leonard Bernstein, *Wonderful Town*

COSTUME DESIGNER
☆ Miles White, *Hazel Flagg*

SCENIC DESIGNER
☆ Raoul Pène Du Bois, *Wonderful Town*

CHOREOGRAPHER
☆ Donald Saddler, *Wonderful Town*

CONDUCTOR AND MUSICAL DIRECTOR
☆ Lehman Engel, *Wonderful Town* and Gilbert and Sullivan Season

STAGE TECHNICIAN
☆ Abe Kurnit, *Wish You Were Here*

SPECIAL AWARDS
☆ Beatrice Lillie
☆ Danny Kaye
☆ Equity Community Theatre

1954

ACTOR (DRAMATIC)
☆ David Wayne, *The Teahouse of the August Moon*

ACTRESS (DRAMATIC)
☆ Audrey Hepburn, *Ondine*

ACTOR, SUPPORTING OR FEATURED (DRAMATIC)
☆ John Kerr, *Tea and Sympathy*

ACTRESS, SUPPORTING OR FEATURED (DRAMATIC)
☆ Jo Van Fleet, *The Trip to Bountiful*

ACTOR (MUSICAL)
☆ Alfred Drake, *Kismet*

ACTRESS (MUSICAL)
☆ Dolores Gray, *Carnival in Flanders*

ACTOR, SUPPORTING OR FEATURED (MUSICAL)
☆ Harry Belafonte, *John Murray Anderson's Almanac*

ACTRESS, SUPPORTING OR FEATURED (MUSICAL)
☆ Gwen Verdon, *Can-Can*

PLAY
☆ *The Teahouse of the August Moon* by John Patrick

PRODUCER (DRAMATIC)
☆ Maurice Evans and George Schaefer, *The Teahouse of the August Moon*

AUTHOR (DRAMATIC)
☆ John Patrick, *The Teahouse of the August Moon*

DIRECTOR
☆ Alfred Lunt, *Ondine*

MUSICAL
☆ *Kismet*. Book by Charles Lederer and Luther Davis, music by Alexander Borodin, adapted and with lyrics by Robert Wright and George Forrest

PRODUCER (MUSICAL)
☆ Charles Lederer, *Kismet*

AUTHOR (MUSICAL)
☆ Charles Lederer and Luther Davis, *Kismet*

COMPOSER
☆ Alexander Borodin, *Kismet*

COSTUME DESIGNER
☆ Richard Whorf, *Ondine*

SCENIC DESIGNER
☆ Peter Larkin, *Ondine* and *The Teahouse of the August Moon*

CHOREOGRAPHER
☆ Michael Kidd, *Can-Can*

MUSICAL CONDUCTOR
☆ Louis Adrian, *Kismet*

STAGE TECHNICIAN
☆ John Davis, *Picnic*

1955

ACTOR (DRAMATIC)
☆ Alfred Lunt, *Quadrille*

ACTRESS (DRAMATIC)
☆ Nancy Kelly, *The Bad Seed*

ACTOR, SUPPORTING OR FEATURED (DRAMATIC)
☆ Francis L. Sullivan, *Witness for the Prosecution*

ACTRESS, SUPPORTING OR FEATURED (DRAMATIC)
☆ Patricia Jessel, *Witness for the Prosecution*

ACTOR (MUSICAL)
☆ Walter Slezak, *Fanny*

ACTRESS (MUSICAL)
☆ Mary Martin, *Peter Pan*

ACTOR, SUPPORTING OR FEATURED (MUSICAL)
☆ Cyril Ritchard, *Peter Pan*

ACTRESS, SUPPORTING OR FEATURED (MUSICAL)
☆ Carol Haney, *The Pajama Game*

PLAY
☆ *The Desperate Hours* by Joseph Hayes

PRODUCERS (DRAMATIC)
☆ Howard Erskine and Joseph Hayes, *The Desperate Hours*

AUTHOR (DRAMATIC)
☆ Joseph Hayes, *The Desperate Hours*

DIRECTOR
☆ Robert Montgomery, *The Desperate Hours*

MUSICAL
☆ *The Pajama Game*. Book by George Abbott and Richard Bissell, music and lyrics by Richard Adler and Jerry Ross

PRODUCERS (MUSICAL)
☆ Federick Brisson, Robert Griffith, and Harold S. Prince, *The Pajama Game*

AUTHORS (MUSICAL)
☆ George Abbott and Richard Bissell, *The Pajama Game*

COMPOSER AND LYRICIST
☆ Richard Adler and Jerry Ross, *The Pajama Game*

COSTUME DESIGNER
☆ Cecil Beaton, *Quadrille*

SCENIC DESIGNER
☆ Oliver Messel, *House of Flowers*

CHOREOGRAPHER
☆ Bob Fosse, *The Pajama Game*

CONDUCTOR AND MUSICAL DIRECTOR
☆ Thomas Schippers, *The Saint of Bleecker Street*

STAGE TECHNICIAN
☆ Richard Rodda, *Peter Pan*

SPECIAL AWARD
☆ Proscenium Productions

1956

ACTOR (DRAMATIC)
Ben Gazzara, A Hatful of Rain
Boris Karloff, The Lark
☆ Paul Muni, Inherit the Wind
Michael Redgrave, Tiger at the Gates
Edward G. Robinson, Middle of the Night

ACTRESS (DRAMATIC)
Barbara Bel Geddes, Cat on a Hot Tin Roof
Gladys Cooper, The Chalk Garden
Ruth Gordon, The Matchmaker
☆ Julie Harris, The Lark
Siobhan McKenna, The Chalk Garden
Susan Strasberg, The Diary of Anne Frank

ACTOR, SUPPORTING OR FEATURED (DRAMATIC)
☆ Ed Begley, Inherit the Wind
Anthony Franciosa, A Hatful of Rain
Andy Griffith, No Time for Sergeants
Anthony Quayle, Tamburlaine the Great
Fritz Weaver, The Chalk Garden

ACTRESS, SUPPORTING OR FEATURED (DRAMATIC)
Diane Cilento, Tiger at the Gates
Anne Jackson, Middle of the Night
☆ Una Merkel, The Ponder Heart
Elaine Stritch, Bus Stop

ACTOR (MUSICAL)
Stephen Douglass, Damn Yankees
William Johnson, Pipe Dream
☆ Ray Walston, Damn Yankees

ACTRESS (MUSICAL)
Carol Channing, The Vamp
☆ Gwen Verdon, Damn Yankees
Nancy Walker, Phoenix '55

ACTOR, SUPPORTING OR FEATURED (MUSICAL)
☆ Russ Brown, Damn Yankees

Mike Kellin, *Pipe Dream*
Will Mahoney, City Center *Finian's Rainbow*
Scott Merrill, *The Threepenny Opera*

ACTRESS, SUPPORTING OR FEATURED (MUSICAL)
Rae Allen, *Damn Yankees*
Pat Carroll, *Catch a Star*
☆ Lotte Lenya, *The Threepenny Opera*
Judy Tyler, *Pipe Dream*

PLAY
Bus Stop by William Inge. Produced by Robert Whitehead and
  Roger L. Stevens
Cat on a Hot Tin Roof by Tennessee Williams. Produced by The
  Playwrights' Company
☆ *The Diary of Anne Frank* by Frances Goodrich and Albert
  Hackett. Produced by Kermit Bloomgarden
Tiger at the Gates by Jean Giraudoux, adapted by Christopher Fry.
  Produced by Robert L. Joseph, The Playwrights' Company,
  and Henry M. Margolis
The Chalk Garden by Enid Bagnold. Produced by Irene Mayer
  Selznick

AUTHORS (DRAMATIC)
☆ Frances Goodrich and Albert Hackett, *The Diary of Anne Frank*

PRODUCER (DRAMATIC)
☆ Kermit Bloomgarden, *The Diary of Anne Frank*

DIRECTOR
Joseph Anthony, *The Lark*
Harold Clurman, *Bus Stop* / *Pipe Dream* / *Tiger at the Gates*
☆ Tyrone Guthrie, ☆ *The Matchmaker* / *Six Characters in Search of an
  Author* / *Tamburlaine the Great*
Garson Kanin, *The Diary of Anne Frank*
Elia Kazan, *Cat on a Hot Tin Roof*
Albert Marre, *The Chalk Garden*
Herman Shumlin, *Inherit the Wind*

MUSICAL
☆ *Damn Yankees* by George Abbott and Douglass Wallop. Music
  by Richard Adler and Jerry Ross. Produced by Frederick
  Brisson, Robert Griffith, and Harold S. Prince in association
  with Albert B. Taylor
Pipe Dream. Book and lyrics by Oscar Hammerstein II, music by
  Richard Rodgers. Produced by Rodgers and Hammerstein

Authors (Musical)
☆ George Abbott and Douglass Wallop, *Damn Yankees*

Producers (Musical)
☆ Frederick Brisson, Robert Griffith, and Harold S. Prince in association with Albert B. Taylor, *Damn Yankees*

Composer and Lyricist
☆ Richard Adler and Jerry Ross, *Damn Yankees*

Conductor and Musical Director
Salvatore Dell'Isola, *Pipe Dream*
☆ Hal Hastings, *Damn Yankees*
Milton Rosenstock, *The Vamp*

Scenic Designer
Boris Aronson, *The Diary of Anne Frank / Bus Stop / Once Upon a Tailor / A View from the Bridge*
Ben Edwards, *The Ponder Heart / Someone Waiting / The Honeys*
☆ Peter Larkin, *Inherit the Wind / No Time for Sergeants*
Jo Mielziner, *Cat on a Hot Tin Roof / The Lark / Middle of the Night / Pipe Dream*
Raymond Sovey, *The Great Sebastians*

Costume Designer
Mainbocher, *The Great Sebastians*
☆ Alvin Colt, *The Lark / Phoenix '55 /* ☆ *Pipe Dream*
Helene Pons, *The Diary of Anne Frank / Heavenly Twins / A View from the Bridge*

Choreographer
Robert Alton, *The Vamp*
☆ Bob Fosse, *Damn Yankees*
Boris Runanin, *Phoenix '55 / Pipe Dream*
Anna Sokolow, *Red Roses for Me*

Stage Technician
Larry Bland, carpenter, *Middle of the Night / The Ponder Heart / Porgy and Bess*
☆ Harry Green, electrician and sound man, *Middle of the Night / Damn Yankees*

Special Awards
☆ *The Threepenny Opera*
☆ The Theatre Collection of the N.Y. Public Library

1957

ACTOR (DRAMATIC)
Maurice Evans, *The Apple Cart*
Wilfred Hyde-White, *The Reluctant Debutante*
☆ Fredric March, *Long Day's Journey Into Night*
Eric Portman, *Separate Tables*
Ralph Richardson, *The Waltz Of The Toreadors*
Cyril Ritchard, *A Visit To A Small Planet*

ACTRESS (DRAMATIC)
Florence Eldridge, *Long Day's Journey Into Night*
☆ Margaret Leighton, *Separate Tables*
Rosalind Russell, *Auntie Mame*
Sybil Thorndike, *The Potting Shed*

ACTOR, SUPPORTING OR FEATURED (DRAMATIC)
☆ Frank Conroy, *The Potting Shed*
Eddie Mayehoff, *A Visit To A Small Planet*
William Podmore, *Separate Tables*
Jason Robards, Jr., *Long Day's Journey Into Night*

ACTRESS, SUPPORTING OR FEATURED (DRAMATIC)
☆ Peggy Cass, *Auntie Mame*
Anna Massey, *The Reluctant Debutante*
Beryl Measor, *Separate Tables*
Mildred Natwick, *The Waltz Of The Toreadors*
Phyllis Neilson-Terry, *Separate Tables*
Diana Van Der Vlis, *The Happiest Millionaire*

ACTOR (MUSICAL)
☆ Rex Harrison, *My Fair Lady*
Fernando Lamas, *Happy Hunting*
Robert Weede, *The Most Happy Fella*

ACTRESS (MUSICAL)
Julie Andrews, *My Fair Lady*
☆ Judy Holliday, *Bells Are Ringing*
Ethel Merman, *Happy Hunting*

ACTOR, SUPPORTING OR FEATURED (MUSICAL)
☆ Sydney Chaplin, *Bells Are Ringing*
Robert Coote, *My Fair Lady*
Stanley Holloway, *My Fair Lady*

ACTRESS, SUPPORTING OR FEATURED (MUSICAL)
☆ Edith Adams, *Li'l Abner*

Virginia Gibson, *Happy Hunting*
Irra Petina, *Candide*
Jo Sullivan, *The Most Happy Fella*

PLAY

☆ *Long Day's Journey Into Night* by Eugene O'Neill. Produced by
   Leigh Connell, Theodore Mann, and José Quintero
Separate Tables by Terence Rattigan. Produced by The Producers
   Theatre and Hecht-Lancaster
The Potting Shed by Graham Greene. Produced by Carmen
   Capalbo and Stanley Chase
The Waltz Of The Toreadors by Jean Anouilh, translated by Lucienne
   Hill. Produced by The Producers Theatre (Robert Whitehead)

AUTHOR (DRAMATIC)

☆ Eugene O'Neill, *Long Day's Journey Into Night*

PRODUCER (DRAMATIC)

☆ Leigh Connell, Theodore Mann and José Quintero, *Long Day's
   Journey Into Night*

DIRECTOR

Joseph Anthony, *A Clearing in the Woods / The Most Happy Fella*
Harold Clurman, *The Waltz of the Toreadors*
Peter Glenville, *Separate Tables*
☆ Moss Hart, *My Fair Lady*
José Quintero, *Long Day's Journey Into Night*

MUSICAL

Bells Are Ringing. Book and lyrics by Betty Comden and Adolph
   Green, music by Jule Styne. Produced by The Theatre Guild
Candide. Book by Lillian Hellman, music by Leonard Bernstein,
   lyrics by Richard Wilbur. Produced by Ethel Linder Reiner in
   association with Lester Osterman, Jr.
☆ *My Fair Lady*. Book and lyrics by Alan Jay Lerner, music by
   Frederick Loewe. Produced by Herman Levin
The Most Happy Fella. Book, music, and lyrics by Frank Loesser.
   Produced by Kermit Bloomgarden and Lynn Loesser

AUTHOR (MUSICAL)

☆ Alan Jay Lerner, *My Fair Lady*

PRODUCER (MUSICAL)

☆ Herman Levin, *My Fair Lady*

COMPOSER

☆ Frederick Loewe, *My Fair Lady*

CONDUCTOR AND MUSICAL DIRECTOR
☆ Franz Allers, *My Fair Lady*
Herbert Greene, *The Most Happy Fella*
Samuel Krachmalnick, *Candide*

SCENIC DESIGNER
Boris Aronson, *A Hole In The Head / Small War on Murray Hill*
Ben Edwards, *The Waltz Of The Toreadors*
George Jenkins, *The Happiest Millionaire / Too Late The Phalarope*
Donald Oenslager, *Major Barbara*
☆ Oliver Smith, *A Clearing in the Woods / Candide / Auntie Mame /*
    ☆ *My Fair Lady / Eugenia / A Visit To A Small Planet*

COSTUME DESIGNER
☆ Cecil Beaton, *Little Glass Clock* / ☆ *My Fair Lady*
Alvin Colt, *Li'l Abner / The Sleeping Prince*
Dorothy Jeakins, *Major Barbara / Too Late The Phalarope*
Irene Sharaff, *Candide / Happy Hunting / Shangri La / Small War on
    Murray Hill*

CHOREOGRAPHER
Hanya Holm, *My Fair Lady*
☆ Michael Kidd, *Li'l Abner*
Dania Krupska, *The Most Happy Fella*
Jerome Robbins and Bob Fosse, *Bells Are Ringing*

STAGE TECHNICIAN
Thomas Fitzgerald, sound man, *Long Day's Journey Into Night*
Joseph Harbach, carpenter, *Auntie Mame*
☆ Howard McDonald, (Posthumous), carpenter, *Major Barbara*

SPECIAL AWARDS
☆ American Shakespeare Festival
☆ Jean-Louis Barrault—French Repertory
☆ Robert Russell Bennett
☆ William Hammerstein
☆ Paul Shyre

1958

ACTOR (DRAMATIC)
☆ Ralph Bellamy, *Sunrise At Campobello*
Richard Burton, *Time Remembered*
Hugh Griffith, *Look Homeward, Angel*
Laurence Olivier, *The Entertainer*

Anthony Perkins, *Look Homeward, Angel*
Peter Ustinov, *Romanoff and Juliet*
Emlyn Williams, *A Boy Growing Up*

ACTRESS (DRAMATIC)
Wendy Hiller, *A Moon For The Misbegotten*
Eugenie Leontovich, *The Cave Dwellers*
☆ Helen Hayes, *Time Remembered*
Siobhan McKenna, *The Rope Dancers*
Mary Ure, *Look Back In Anger*
Jo Van Fleet, *Look Homeward, Angel*

ACTOR, SUPPORTING OR FEATURED (DRAMATIC)
☆ Henry Jones, *Sunrise At Campobello*

ACTRESS, SUPPORTING OR FEATURED (DRAMATIC)
☆ Anne Bancroft, *Two For The Seesaw*

ACTOR (MUSICAL)
Ricardo Montalban, *Jamaica*
☆ Robert Preston, *The Music Man*
Eddie Foy, Jr., *Rumple*
Tony Randall, *Oh, Captain!*

ACTRESS (MUSICAL)
☆ Thelma Ritter, *New Girl In Town*
Lena Horne, *Jamaica*
Beatrice Lillie, *Ziegfeld Follies*
☆ Gwen Verdon, *New Girl In Town*

ACTOR, SUPPORTING OR FEATURED (MUSICAL)
☆ David Burns, *The Music Man*

ACTRESS, SUPPORTING OR FEATURED (MUSICAL)
☆ Barbara Cook, *The Music Man*

PLAY
The Rope Dancers by Morton Wishengrad
Two For The Seesaw by William Gibson
Time Remembered by Jean Anouilh. English version by Patricia
  Moyes
The Dark at the Top of the Stairs by William Inge
Look Back In Anger by John Osborne
Romanoff and Juliet by Peter Ustinov
☆ *Sunrise At Campobello* by Dore Schary

AUTHOR (DRAMATIC)
☆ Dore Schary, *Sunrise At Campobello*

PRODUCERS (DRAMATIC)
☆ Lawrence Langner, Theresa Helburn, Armina Marshall, and Dore Schary, *Sunrise At Campobello*

DIRECTOR (DRAMATIC)
☆ Vincent J. Donehue, *Sunrise At Campobello*

MUSICAL
West Side Story. Book by Arthur Laurents, music by Leonard Bernstein, lyrics by Stephen Sondheim

New Girl In Town. Book by George Abbott, music and lyrics by Bob Merrill

☆ *The Music Man.* Book by Meredith Willson and Franklin Lacey, music and lyrics by Meredith Willson

Oh, Captain! Book by Al Morgan and José Ferrer, music and lyrics by Jay Livingston and Ray Evans

Jamaica. Book by E. Y. Harburg and Fred Saidy, music by Harold Arlen, lyrics by E. Y. Harburg

AUTHOR (MUSICAL)
☆ Meredith Willson and Franklin Lacey, *The Music Man*

PRODUCER (MUSICAL)
☆ Kermit Bloomgarden, Herbert Greene, and Frank Productions, *The Music Man*

COMPOSER AND LYRICIST
☆ Meredith Willson, *The Music Man*

CONDUCTOR AND MUSICAL DIRECTOR
☆ Herbert Greene, *The Music Man*

SCENIC DESIGNER
☆ Oliver Smith, *West Side Story*

COSTUME DESIGNER
☆ Motley, *The First Gentleman*

CHOREOGRAPHER
☆ Jerome Robbins, *West Side Story*

STAGE TECHNICIAN
☆ Harry Romar, *Time Remembered*

SPECIAL AWARDS
☆ New York Shakespeare Festival
☆ Mrs. Martin Beck

1959

ACTOR (DRAMATIC)
Cedric Hardwicke, A *Majority of One*
Alfred Lunt, *The Visit*
Christopher Plummer, *J. B.*
Cyril Ritchard, *The Pleasure of His Company*
☆ Jason Robards, Jr., *The Disenchanted*
Robert Stephens, *Epitaph for George Dillon*

ACTRESS (DRAMATIC)
☆ Gertrude Berg, A *Majority of One*
Claudette Colbert, *The Marriage-Go-Round*
Lynn Fontanne, *The Visit*
Kim Stanley, A *Touch of the Poet*
Maureen Stapleton, *The Cold Wind and the Warm*

ACTOR, SUPPORTING OR FEATURED (DRAMATIC)
Marc Connelly, *Tall Story*
George Grizzard, *The Disenchanted*
Walter Matthau, *Once More, With Feeling*
Robert Morse, *Say, Darling*
☆ Charlie Ruggles, *The Pleasure of His Company*
George Scott, *Comes a Day*

ACTRESS, SUPPORTING OR FEATURED (DRAMATIC)
Maureen Delany, *God and Kate Murphy*
Dolores Hart, *The Pleasure of His Company*
☆ Julie Newmar, *The Marriage-Go-Round*
Nan Martin, *J. B.*
Bertrice Reading, *Requiem for a Nun*

ACTOR (MUSICAL)
Larry Blyden, *Flower Drum Song*
☆ Richard Kiley, *Redhead*

ACTRESS (MUSICAL)
Miyoshi Umeki, *Flower Drum Song*
☆ Gwen Verdon, *Redhead*

ACTOR, SUPPORTING OR FEATURED (MUSICAL)
☆ Russell Nype, *Goldilocks*
Leonard Stone, *Redhead*
☆ Cast of *La Plume de Ma Tante*

ACTRESS, SUPPORTING OR FEATURED (MUSICAL)
Julienne Marie, *Whoop-Up*

☆ Pat Stanley, *Goldilocks*
☆ Cast of *La Plume de Ma Tante*

PLAY

A *Touch of the Poet* by Eugene O'Neill. Produced by The Producers
    Theatre, Robert Whitehead, and Roger L. Stevens
Epitaph for George Dillon by John Osborne and Anthony Creighton.
    Produced by David Merrick and Joshua Logan
☆ J. B. by Archibald MacLeish. Produced by Alfred de Liagre, Jr.
The Disenchanted by Budd Schulberg and Harvey Breit. Produced
    by William Darrid and Eleanor Saidenberg
The Visit by Friedrich Duerrenmatt, adapted by Maurice Valency.
    Produced by the Producers Theatre

AUTHOR (DRAMATIC)

☆ Archibald MacLeish, *J. B.*

PRODUCER (DRAMATIC)

☆ Alfred de Liagre, Jr., *J. B.*

DIRECTOR

Peter Brook, *The Visit*
Robert Dhéry, *La Plume de Ma Tante*
William Gaskill, *Epitaph for George Dillon*
Peter Glenville, *Rashomon*
☆ Elia Kazan, *J. B.*
Cyril Ritchard, *The Pleasure of His Company*
Dore Schary, *A Majority of One*

MUSICAL

Flower Drum Song. Book by Oscar Hammerstein II and Joseph
    Fields, lyrics by Oscar Hammerstein II, music by Richard
    Rodgers
La Plume de Ma Tante. Written, devised, and directed by Robert
    Dhery, music by Gerard Calvi, English lyrics by Ross Parker.
    (David Merrick and Joseph Kipness present the Jack Hylton
    Production)
☆ *Redhead* by Herbert and Dorothy Fields, Sidney Sheldon, and
    David Shaw, music by Albert Hague, lyrics by Dorothy Fields

AUTHORS (MUSICAL)

☆ Herbert and Dorothy Fields, Sidney Sheldon, and David
    Shaw, *Redhead*

PRODUCERS (MUSICAL)

☆ Robert Fryer and Lawrence Carr, *Redhead*

COMPOSER
☆ Albert Hague, *Redhead*

CONDUCTOR AND MUSICAL DIRECTOR
Jay Blackston, *Redhead*
☆ Salvatore Dell'Isola, *Flower Drum Song*
Lehman Engel, *Goldilocks*
Gershon Kingsley, *La Plume de Ma Tante*

SCENIC DESIGNER
Boris Aronson, J. B.
Ballou, *The Legend of Lizzie*
Ben Edwards, *Jane Eyre*
Oliver Messel, *Rashomon*
☆ Donald Oenslager, *A Majority of One*
Teo Otto, *The Visit*

COSTUME DESIGNER
Castillo, *Goldilocks*
Dorothy Jeakins, *The World of Suzie Wong*
Oliver Messel, *Rashomon*
Irene Sharaff, *Flower Drum Song*
☆ Rouben Ter-Arutunian, *Redhead*

CHOREOGRAPHER
Agnes de Mille, *Goldilocks*
☆ Bob Fosse, *Redhead*
Carol Haney, *Flower Drum Song*
Onna White, *Whoop-Up*

STAGE TECHNICIAN
Thomas Fitzgerald, *Who Was That Lady I Saw You With?*
Edward Flynn, *The Most Happy Fella* (City Center Revival)
☆ Sam Knapp, *The Music Man*

SPECIAL AWARDS
☆ John Gielgud
☆ Howard Lindsay and Russel Crouse

The 1960s

"There is something very special about having your work acknowledged by your peers. It is a milestone to work for, and the 'first time' something like this happens to you it is deeply satisfying."

Joel Grey

"The curious thing about awards is that one receives them for work one does not expect to receive them for, and does not receive them for work one does. For instance, I received the Tony® for 'Hallelujah, Baby!'— and not for 'Gypsy!' But, the Tony®, which stands for excellence in the theatre, is an honor whenever it comes!"

Jule Styne

1960

ACTOR (DRAMATIC)
☆ Melvyn Douglas, *The Best Man*
Lee Tracy, *The Best Man*
Jason Robards, Jr., *Toys in the Attic*
Sidney Poitier, *A Raisin in the Sun*
George C. Scott, *The Andersonville Trial*

ACTRESS (DRAMATIC)
☆ Anne Bancroft, *The Miracle Worker*
Margaret Leighton, *Much Ado About Nothing*
Claudia McNeil, *A Raisin in the Sun*
Geraldine Page, *Sweet Bird of Youth*
Maureen Stapleton, *Toys in the Attic*
Irene Worth, *Toys in the Attic*

ACTOR, SUPPORTING OR FEATURED (DRAMATIC)
Warren Beatty, *A Loss of Roses*
Harry Guardino, *One More River*
☆ Roddy McDowall, *The Fighting Cock*
Rip Torn, *Sweet Bird of Youth*
Lawrence Winters, *The Long Dream*

ACTRESS, SUPPORTING OR FEATURED (DRAMATIC)
Leora Dana, *The Best Man*
Jane Fonda, *There Was a Little Girl*
Sarah Marshall, *Goodbye, Charlie*
Juliet Mills, *Five Finger Exercise*
☆ Anne Revere, *Toys in the Attic*

ACTOR (MUSICAL)
☆ Jackie Gleason, *Take Me Along*
Robert Morse, *Take Me Along*
Walter Pidgeon, *Take Me Along*
Andy Griffith, *Destry Rides Again*
Anthony Perkins, *Greenwillow*

ACTRESS (MUSICAL)
Carol Burnett, *Once Upon a Mattress*
Dolores Gray, *Destry Rides Again*
Eileen Herlie, *Take Me Along*
☆ Mary Martin, *The Sound of Music*
Ethel Merman, *Gypsy*

ACTOR, SUPPORTING OR FEATURED (MUSICAL)
Theodore Bikel, *The Sound of Music*
Kurt Kasznar, *The Sound of Music*
☆ Tom Bosley, *Fiorello!*
Howard Da Silva, *Fiorello!*
Jack Klugman, *Gypsy*

ACTRESS, SUPPORTING OR FEATURED (MUSICAL)
Sandra Church, *Gypsy*
Pert Kelton, *Greenwillow*
☆ Patricia Neway, *The Sound of Music*
Lauri Peters, *The Sound of Music*
The Children, *The Sound of Music*

PLAY
A *Raisin in the Sun* by Lorraine Hansberry. Produced by Philip
   Rose and David J. Cogan
The Best Man by Gore Vidal. Produced by The Playwrights'
   Company
☆ *The Miracle Worker* by William Gibson. Produced by Fred Coe
The Tenth Man by Paddy Chayefsky. Produced by Saint-Subber
   and Arthur Cantor
Toys in the Attic by Lillian Hellman. Produced by Kermit
   Bloomgarden

AUTHOR (DRAMATIC)
☆ William Gibson, *The Miracle Worker*

PRODUCER (DRAMATIC)
☆ Fred Coe, *The Miracle Worker*

DIRECTOR (DRAMATIC)
Joseph Anthony, *The Best Man*
Tyrone Guthrie, *The Tenth Man*
Elia Kazan, *Sweet Bird of Youth*
☆ Arthur Penn, *The Miracle Worker*
Lloyd Richards, A *Raisin in the Sun*

MUSICAL
☆ *Fiorello!* by Jerome Weidman and George Abbott. Lyrics by
   Sheldon Harnick, music by Jerry Bock. Produced by Robert E.
   Griffith and Harold S. Prince
Gypsy by Arthur Laurents. Lyrics by Stephen Sondheim, music by
   Jule Styne. Produced by David Merrick and Leland Hayward
Once Upon a Mattress. Book by Jay Thompson, Marshall Barer, and
   Dean Fuller, lyrics by Marshall Barer, music by Mary Rodgers.

Produced by T. Edward Hambleton, Norris Houghton, and William and Jean Eckart

Take Me Along. Book by Joseph Stein and Robert Russell, lyrics and music by Bob Merrill. Produced by David Merrick

☆ *The Sound of Music* by Howard Lindsay and Russel Crouse. Lyrics by Oscar Hammerstein II, music by Richard Rodgers. Produced by Leland Hayward, Richard Halliday, and Rodgers and Hammerstein

AUTHORS (MUSICAL)

☆ Jerome Weidman and George Abbott, *Fiorello!*
☆ Howard Lindsay and Russel Crouse, *The Sound of Music*

PRODUCER (MUSICAL)

☆ Robert Griffith and Harold Prince, *Fiorello!*
☆ Leland Hayward and Richard Halliday, *The Sound of Music*

DIRECTOR (MUSICAL)

☆ George Abbott, *Fiorello!*
Vincent J. Donehue, *The Sound of Music*
Peter Glenville, *Take Me Along*
Michael Kidd, *Destry Rides Again*
Jerome Robbins, *Gypsy*

COMPOSERS

☆ Jerry Bock, *Fiorello!*
☆ Richard Rodgers, *The Sound of Music*

CONDUCTOR AND MUSICAL DIRECTOR

Abba Bogin, *Greenwillow*
☆ Frederick Dvonch, *The Sound of Music*
Lehman Engel, *Take Me Along*
Hal Hastings, *Fiorello!*
Milton Rosenstock, *Gypsy*

SCENIC DESIGNER (DRAMATIC)

Will Steven Armstrong, *Caligula*
☆ Howard Bay, *Toys in the Attic*
David Hays, *The Tenth Man*
George Jenkins, *The Miracle Worker*
Jo Mielziner, *The Best Man*

SCENIC DESIGNER (MUSICAL)

Cecil Beaton, *Saratoga*
William and Jean Eckart, *Fiorello!*
Peter Larkin, *Greenwillow*
Jo Mielziner, *Gypsy*
☆ Oliver Smith, *The Sound of Music*

COSTUME DESIGNER
☆ Cecil Beaton, *Saratoga*
Alvin Colt, *Greenwillow*
Raoul Pène Du Bois, *Gypsy*
Miles White, *Take Me Along*

CHOREOGRAPHER
Peter Gennaro, *Fiorello!*
☆ Michael Kidd, *Destry Rides Again*
Joe Layton, *Greenwillow*
Lee Scott, *Happy Town*
Onna White, *Take Me Along*

STAGE TECHNICIAN
Al Alloy, chief electrician, *Take Me Along*
James Orr, chief electrician, *Greenwillow*
☆ John Walters, chief carpenter, *The Miracle Worker*

SPECIAL AWARDS
☆ John D. Rockefeller III
☆ James Thurber and Burgess Meredith, A *Thurber Carnival*

1961

ACTOR (DRAMATIC)
Hume Cronyn, *Big Fish, Little Fish*
Sam Levene, *The Devil's Advocate*
☆ Zero Mostel, *Rhinoceros*
Anthony Quinn, *Becket*

ACTRESS (DRAMATIC)
Tallulah Bankhead, *Midgie Purvis*
Barbara Baxley, *Period of Adjustment*
Barbara Bel Geddes, *Mary, Mary*
☆ Joan Plowright, A *Taste of Honey*

ACTOR, SUPPORTING OR FEATURED (DRAMATIC)
Philip Bosco, *The Rape of the Belt*
Eduardo Ciannelli, *The Devil's Advocate*
☆ Martin Gabel, *Big Fish, Little Fish*
George Grizzard, *Big Fish, Little Fish*

ACTRESS, SUPPORTING OR FEATURED (DRAMATIC)
☆ Colleen Dewhurst, *All the Way Home*
Eileen Heckart, *Invitation to a March*

Tresa Hughes, *The Devil's Advocate*
Rosemary Murphy, *Period of Adjustment*

ACTOR (MUSICAL)
☆ Richard Burton, *Camelot*
Phil Silvers, *Do Re Mi*
Maurice Evans, *Tenderloin*

ACTRESS (MUSICAL)
Julie Andrews, *Camelot*
Carol Channing, *Show Girl*
☆ Elizabeth Seal, *Irma la Douce*
Nancy Walker, *Do Re Mi*

ACTOR, SUPPORTING OR FEATURED (MUSICAL)
Clive Revill, *Irma la Douce*
Dick Gautier, *Bye, Bye Birdie*
Ron Husmann, *Tenderloin*
☆ Dick Van Dyke, *Bye, Bye Birdie*

ACTRESS, SUPPORTING OR FEATURED (MUSICAL)
Nancy Dussault, *Do Re Mi*
☆ Tammy Grimes, *The Unsinkable Molly Brown*
Chita Rivera, *Bye, Bye Birdie*

PLAY
All the Way Home by Tad Mosel. Produced by Fred Coe in association with Arthur Cantor
☆ *Becket* by Jean Anouilh, translated by Lucienne Hill. Produced by David Merrick
The Devil's Advocate by Dore Schary. Produced by Dore Schary
The Hostage by Brendan Behan. Produced by S. Field and Caroline Burke Swann

AUTHOR (DRAMATIC)
☆ Jean Anouilh, *Becket*

PRODUCER (DRAMATIC)
☆ David Merrick, *Becket*

DIRECTOR (DRAMATIC)
Joseph Anthony, *Rhinoceros*
☆ Sir John Gielgud, *Big Fish, Little Fish*
Joan Littlewood, *The Hostage*
Arthur Penn, *All the Way Home*

MUSICAL

☆ *Bye, Bye Birdie*. Book by Michael Stewart, music by Charles Strouse, lyrics by Lee Adams. Produced by Edward Padula in association with L. Slade Brown

Do Re Mi. Book by Garson Kanin, music by Jules Styne, lyrics by Betty Comden and Adolph Green. Produced by David Merrick

Irma la Douce. Book and lyrics by Alexandre Breffort, music by Marguerite Monnot. English book and lyrics by Julian More, David Heneker, and Monty Norman. Produced by David Merrick in association with Donald Albery and H. M. Tennent, Ltd.

AUTHOR (MUSICAL)

☆ Michael Stewart, *Bye, Bye Birdie*

PRODUCER (MUSICAL)

☆ Edward Padula, *Bye, Bye Birdie*

DIRECTOR (MUSICAL)

Peter Brook, *Irma la Douce*
☆ Gower Champion, *Bye, Bye Birdie*
Garson Kanin, *Do Re Mi*

CONDUCTOR AND MUSICAL DIRECTOR

☆ Franz Allers, *Camelot*
Pembroke Davenport, *13 Daughters*
Stanley Lebowsky, *Irma la Douce*
Elliot Lawrence, *Bye, Bye Birdie*

SCENIC DESIGNER (DRAMATIC)

Roger Furse, *Duel of Angels*
David Hays, *All the Way Home*
Jo Mielziner, *The Devil's Advocate*
☆ Oliver Smith, *Becket*
Rouben Ter-Arutunian, *Advise and Consent*

SCENIC DESIGNER (MUSICAL)

George Jenkins, *13 Daughters*
Robert Randolph, *Bye, Bye Birdie*
☆ Oliver Smith, *Camelot*

COSTUME DESIGNER (DRAMATIC)

Theoni V. Aldredge, *The Devil's Advocate*
☆ Motley, *Becket*
Raymond Sovey, *All the Way Home*

COSTUME DESIGNER (MUSICAL)
☆ Adrian and Tony Duquette, *Camelot*
Rolf Gerard, *Irma la Douce*
Cecil Beaton, *Tenderloin*

CHOREOGRAPHER
☆ Gower Champion, *Bye, Bye Birdie*
Onna White, *Irma la Douce*

STAGE TECHNICIAN
☆ Teddy Van Bemmel, *Becket*

SPECIAL AWARDS
☆ David Merrick
☆ The Theatre Guild

1962

ACTOR (DRAMATIC)
Fredric March, *Gideon*
John Mills, *Ross*
Donald Pleasence, *The Caretaker*
☆ Paul Scofield, *A Man for All Seasons*

ACTRESS (DRAMATIC)
Gladys Cooper, *A Passage to India*
Colleen Dewhurst, *Great Day in the Morning*
☆ Margaret Leighton, *Night of the Iguana*
Kim Stanley, *A Far Country*

ACTOR, SUPPORTING OR FEATURED (DRAMATIC)
Godfrey M. Cambridge, *Purlie Victorious*
Joseph Campanella, *A Gift of Time*
☆ Walter Matthau, *A Shot in the Dark*
Paul Sparer, *Ross*

ACTRESS, SUPPORTING OR FEATURED (DRAMATIC)
☆ Elizabeth Ashley, *Take Her, She's Mine*
Zohra Lampert, *Look: We've Come Through*
Janet Margolin, *Daughter of Silence*
Pat Stanley, *Sunday in New York*

ACTOR (MUSICAL)
Ray Bolger, *All American*
Alfred Drake, *Kean*
Richard Kiley, *No Strings*
☆ Robert Morse, *How to Succeed in Business Without Really Trying*

ACTRESS (MUSICAL)
☆ Anna Maria Alberghetti, *Carnival*
☆ Diahann Carroll, *No Strings*
Molly Picon, *Milk and Honey*
Elaine Stritch, *Sail Away*

ACTOR, SUPPORTING OR FEATURED (MUSICAL)
Orson Bean, *Subways Are for Sleeping*
Severn Darden, *From the Second City*
Pierre Olaf, *Carnival*
☆ Charles Nelson Reilly, *How to Succeed in Business Without Really Trying*

ACTRESS, SUPPORTING OR FEATURED (MUSICAL)
Elizabeth Allen, *The Gay Life*
Barbara Harris, *From the Second City*
☆ Phyllis Newman, *Subways Are for Sleeping*
Barbra Streisand, *I Can Get It for You Wholesale*

PLAY
☆ *A Man for All Seasons* by Robert Bolt. Produced by Robert Whitehead and Roger L. Stevens
Gideon by Paddy Chayefsky. Produced by Fred Coe and Arthur Cantor
The Caretaker by Harold Pinter. Produced by Roger L. Stevens, Frederick Brisson, and Gilbert Miller
The Night of the Iguana by Tennessee Williams. Produced by Charles Bowden and Viola Rubber

AUTHOR (DRAMATIC)
☆ Robert Bolt, *A Man for All Seasons*

PRODUCER (DRAMATIC)
Charles Bowden and Viola Rubber, *Night of the Iguana*
Fred Coe and Arthur Cantor, *Gideon*
David Merrick, *Ross*
☆ Robert Whitehead and Roger L. Stevens, *A Man for All Seasons*

DIRECTOR (DRAMATIC)
Tyrone Guthrie, *Gideon*
Donald McWhinnie, *The Caretaker*
José Quintero, *Great Day in the Morning*
☆ Noel Willman, *A Man for All Seasons*

MUSICAL
Carnival. Book by Michael Stewart and Helen Deutsch, music and lyrics by Bob Merrill. Produced by David Merrick

☆ *How to Succeed in Business Without Really Trying*. Book by Abe Burrows, Jack Weinstock, and Willie Gilbert, music and lyrics by Frank Loesser. Produced by Cy Feuer and Ernest Martin

Milk and Honey. Book by Don Appell, lyrics and music by Jerry Herman. Produced by Gerard Oestreicher

No Strings. Book by Samuel Taylor, music and lyrics by Richard Rodgers. Produced by Richard Rodgers in association with Samuel Taylor

Author (Musical)
☆ Abe Burrows, Jack Weinstock, and Willie Gilbert, *How to Succeed in Business Without Really Trying*
Michael Stewart and Helen Deutsch, *Carnival*

Producer (Musical)
Helen Bonfils, Haila Stoddard, and Charles Russell, *Sail Away*
☆ Cy Feuer and Ernest Martin, *How to Succeed in Business Without Really Trying*
David Merrick, *Carnival*
Gerard Oestreicher, *Milk and Honey*

Director (Musical)
☆ Abe Burrows, *How to Succeed in Business Without Really Trying*
Gower Champion, *Carnival*
Joe Layton, *No Strings*
Joshua Logan, *All American*

Composer
Richard Adler, *Kwamina*
Jerry Herman, *Milk and Honey*
Frank Loesser, *How to Succeed in Business Without Really Trying*
☆ Richard Rodgers, *No Strings*

Conductor and Musical Director
Pembroke Davenport, *Kean*
Herbert Greene, *The Gay Life*
☆ Elliot Lawrence, *How to Succeed in Business Without Really Trying*
Peter Matz, *No Strings*

Scenic Designer
☆ Will Steven Armstrong, *Carnival*
Rouben Ter-Arutunian, *A Passage to India*
David Hays, *No Strings*
Oliver Smith, *The Gay Life*

Costume Designer
☆ Lucinda Ballard, *The Gay Life*

Donald Brooks, *No Strings*
Motley, *Kwamina*
Miles White, *Milk and Honey*

CHOREOGRAPHER
☆ Agnes de Mille, *Kwamina*
Michael Kidd, *Subways Are for Sleeping*
Dania Krupska, *The Happiest Girl in the World*
☆ Joe Layton, *No Strings*

STAGE TECHNICIAN
Al Alloy, *Ross*
☆ Michael Burns, *A Man for All Seasons*

SPECIAL AWARDS
☆ Brooks Atkinson
☆ Franco Zeffirelli
☆ Richard Rodgers
☆ Richard Rodgers also received the Tony® for *No Strings*

1963

ACTOR (DRAMATIC)
Charles Boyer, *Lord Pengo*
Paul Ford, *Never Too Late*
☆ Arthur Hill, *Who's Afraid of Virginia Woolf?*
Bert Lahr, *The Beauty Part*

ACTRESS (DRAMATIC)
Hermione Baddeley, *The Milk Train Doesn't Stop Here Anymore*
☆ Uta Hagen, *Who's Afraid of Virginia Woolf?*
Margaret Leighton, *Tchin-Tchin*
Claudia McNeill, *Tiger Tiger Burning Bright*

ACTOR, SUPPORTING OR FEATURED (DRAMATIC)
☆ Alan Arkin, *Enter Laughing*
Barry Gordon, *A Thousand Clowns*
Paul Rogers, *Photo Finish*
Frank Silvera, *The Lady of the Camellias*

ACTRESS, SUPPORTING OR FEATURED (DRAMATIC)
☆ Sandy Dennis, *A Thousand Clowns*
Melinda Dillon, *Who's Afraid of Virginia Woolf?*
Alice Ghostley, *The Beauty Part*
Zohra Lampert, *Mother Courage and Her Children*

ACTOR (MUSICAL)
Sid Caesar, *Little Me*
☆ Zero Mostel, *A Funny Thing Happened on the Way to the Forum*
Anthony Newley, *Stop the World—I Want to Get Off*
Clive Revill, *Oliver!*

ACTRESS (MUSICAL)
Georgia Brown, *Oliver!*
Nanette Fabray, *Mr. President*
Sally Ann Howes, *Brigadoon*
☆ Vivien Leigh, *Tovarich*

ACTOR, SUPPORTING OR FEATURED (MUSICAL)
☆ David Burns, *A Funny Thing Happened on the Way to the Forum*
Jack Gilford, *A Funny Thing Happened on the Way to the Forum*
David Jones, *Oliver!*
Swen Swenson, *Little Me*

ACTRESS, SUPPORTING OR FEATURED (MUSICAL)
Ruth Kobart, *A Funny Thing Happened on the Way to the Forum*
Virginia Martin, *Little Me*
☆ Anna Quayle, *Stop the World—I Want to Get Off*
Louise Troy, *Tovarich*

PLAY
A Thousand Clowns by Herb Gardner. Produced by Fred Coe and
   Arthur Cantor
Mother Courage and Her Children by Bertolt Brecht, adapted by Eric
   Bentley. Produced by Cheryl Crawford and Jerome Robbins
Tchin-Tchin by Sidney Michaels. Produced by David Merrick
☆ *Who's Afraid of Virginia Woolf?* by Edward Albee. Produced by
   Theatre 1963, Richard Barr, and Clinton Wilder

PRODUCER (DRAMATIC)
The Actors Studio Theatre, *Strange Interlude*
☆ Richard Barr and Clinton Wilder, Theatre 1963, *Who's Afraid of
   Virginia Woolf?*
Cheryl Crawford and Jerome Robbins, *Mother Courage and Her
   Children*
Paul Vroom, Buff Cobb, and Burry Fredrik, *Too True To Be Good*

DIRECTOR (DRAMATIC)
George Abbott, *Never Too Late*
John Gielgud, *The School for Scandal*
Peter Glenville, *Tchin-Tchin*
☆ Alan Schneider, *Who's Afraid of Virginia Woolf?*

MUSICAL

☆ A *Funny Thing Happened on the Way to the Forum*. Book by Burt Shevelove and Larry Gelbart, music and lyrics by Stephen Sondheim. Produced by Harold Prince

Little Me. Book by Neil Simon, music by Cy Coleman, lyrics by Carolyn Leigh. Produced by Cy Feuer and Ernest Martin

Oliver! Book, music, and lyrics by Lionel Bart. Produced by David Merrick and Donald Albery

Stop the World—I Want to Get Off. Book, music, and lyrics by Leslie Bricusse and Anthony Newley. Produced by David Merrick in association with Bernard Delfont

AUTHOR (MUSICAL)

Lionel Bart, *Oliver!*

Leslie Bricusse and Anthony Newley, *Stop the World—I Want to Get Off*

☆ Burt Shevelove and Larry Gelbart, A *Funny Thing Happened on the Way to the Forum*

Neil Simon, *Little Me*

PRODUCER (MUSICAL)

Cy Feuer and Ernest Martin, *Little Me*

David Merrick and Donald Albery, *Oliver!*

☆ Harold Prince, A *Funny Thing Happened on the Way to the Forum*

DIRECTOR (MUSICAL)

☆ George Abbott, A *Funny Thing Happened on the Way to the Forum*

Peter Coe, *Oliver!*

John Fearnley, *Brigadoon*

Cy Feuer and Bob Fosse, *Little Me*

COMPOSER AND LYRICIST

☆ Lionel Bart, *Oliver!*

Leslie Bricusse and Anthony Newley, *Stop the World—I Want to Get Off*

Cy Coleman and Carolyn Leigh, *Little Me*

Milton Schafer and Ronny Graham, *Bravo Giovanni*

CONDUCTOR AND MUSICAL DIRECTOR

Jay Blackton, *Mr. President*

Anton Coppola, *Bravo Giovanni*

☆ Donald Pippin, *Oliver!*

Julius Rudel, *Brigadoon*

SCENIC DESIGNER

Will Steven Armstrong, *Tchin-Tchin*

☆ Sean Kenny, *Oliver!*

Anthony Powell, *The School for Scandal*

Franco Zeffirelli, *The Lady of the Camellias*

COSTUME DESIGNER
Marcel Escoffier, *The Lady of the Camellias*
Robert Fletcher, *Little Me*
Motley, *Mother Courage and Her Children*
☆ Anthony Powell, *The School for Scandal*

CHOREOGRAPHER
☆ Bob Fosse, *Little Me*
Carol Haney, *Bravo Giovanni*

STAGE TECHNICIAN
☆ Solly Pernick, *Mr. President*
Milton Smith, *Beyond the Fringe*

SPECIAL AWARDS
☆ W. McNeil Lowry
☆ Irving Berlin
☆ Alan Bennett
☆ Peter Cook
☆ Jonathan Miller
☆ Dudley Moore

1964

ACTOR (DRAMATIC)
Richard Burton, *Hamlet*
Albert Finney, *Luther*
☆ Alec Guinness, *Dylan*
Jason Robards, Jr, *After the Fall*

ACTRESS (DRAMATIC) PLAY
Elizabeth Ashley, *Barefoot in the Park*
☆ Sandy Dennis, *Any Wednesday*
Colleen Dewhurst, *The Ballad of the Sad Café*
Julie Harris, *Marathon '33*

ACTOR, SUPPORTING OR FEATURED (DRAMATIC)
Lee Allen, *Marathon '33*
☆ Hume Cronyn, *Hamlet*
Michael Dunn, *The Ballad of the Sad Café*
Larry Gates, *A Case of Libel*

ACTRESS, SUPPORTING OR FEATURED (DRAMATIC)
☆ Barbara Loden, *After the Fall*
Rosemary Murphy, *Any Wednesday*

Kate Reid, *Dylan*
Diana Sands, *Blues for Mister Charlie*

ACTOR (MUSICAL)
Sydney Chaplin, *Funny Girl*
Bob Fosse, *Pal Joey* (City Center revival)
☆ Bert Lahr, *Foxy*
Steve Lawrence, *What Makes Sammy Run*

ACTRESS (MUSICAL)
☆ Carol Channing, *Hello, Dolly!*
Beatrice Lillie, *High Spirits*
Barbra Streisand, *Funny Girl*
Inga Swenson, *110 in the Shade*

ACTOR, SUPPORTING OR FEATURED (MUSICAL)
☆ Jack Cassidy, *She Loves Me*
Will Geer, *110 in the Shade*
Danny Meehan, *Funny Girl*
Charles Nelson Reilly, *Hello, Dolly!*

ACTRESS, SUPPORTING OR FEATURED (MUSICAL)
Julienne Marie, *Foxy*
Kay Medford, *Funny Girl*
☆ Tessie O'Shea, *The Girl Who Came to Supper*
Louise Troy, *High Spirits*

PLAY
The Ballad of the Sad Café by Edward Albee. Produced by Lewis Allen and Ben Edwards
Barefoot in the Park by Neil Simon. Produced by Saint Subber
Dylan by Sidney Michaels. Produced by George W. George and Frank Granat
☆ *Luther* by John Osborne. Produced by David Merrick

AUTHOR (DRAMATIC)
☆ John Osborne, *Luther*

PRODUCER (DRAMATIC)
Lewis Allen and Ben Edwards, *The Ballad of the Sad Café*
George W. George and Frank Granat, *Dylan*
☆ Herman Shumlin, *The Deputy*
Saint Subber, *Barefoot in the Park*

DIRECTOR (DRAMATIC)
June Havoc, *Marathon '33*
☆ Mike Nichols, *Barefoot in the Park*
Alan Schneider, *The Ballad of the Sad Café*
Herman Shumlin, *The Deputy*

MUSICAL

Funny Girl. Book by Isobel Lennart, music by Jule Styne, lyrics by Bob Merrill. Produced by Ray Stark

☆ *Hello, Dolly!* Book by Michael Stewart, music and lyrics by Jerry Herman. Produced by David Merrick

High Spirits. Book, lyrics, and music by Hugh Martin and Timothy Gray. Produced by Lester Osterman, Robert Fletcher, and Richard Horner

She Loves Me. Book by Joe Masteroff, music by Jerry Bock, lyrics by Sheldon Harnick. Produced by Harold Prince in association with Lawrence N. Kasha and Philip C. McKenna

AUTHOR (MUSICAL)

Noel Coward and Harry Kurnitz, *The Girl Who Came to Supper*

Joe Masteroff, *She Loves Me*

Hugh Martin and Timothy Gray, *High Spirits*

☆ Michael Stewart, *Hello, Dolly!*

PRODUCER (MUSICAL)

City Center Light Opera Company, *West Side Story*

☆ David Merrick, *Hello, Dolly!*

Harold Prince, *She Loves Me*

Ray Stark, *Funny Girl*

DIRECTOR (MUSICAL)

Joseph Anthony, *110 in the Shade*

☆ Gower Champion, *Hello, Dolly!*

Noel Coward, *High Spirits*

Harold Prince, *She Loves Me*

COMPOSER AND LYRICIST

☆ Jerry Herman, *Hello, Dolly!*

Hugh Martin and Timothy Gray, *High Spirits*

Harvey Schmidt and Tom Jones, *110 in the Shade*

Jule Styne and Bob Merrill, *Funny Girl*

CONDUCTOR AND MUSICAL DIRECTOR

☆ Shepard Coleman, *Hello, Dolly!*

Lehman Engel, *What Makes Sammy Run?*

Charles Jaffe, *West Side Story*

Fred Werner, *High Spirits*

SCENIC DESIGNER

Raoul Pène Du Bois, *The Student Gypsy*

Ben Edwards, *The Ballad of the Sad Café*

David Hays, *Marco Millions*

☆ Oliver Smith, *Hello, Dolly!*

COSTUMER DESIGNER
Irene Sharaff, *The Girl Who Came to Supper*
Beni Montresor, *Marco Millions*
Rouben Ter-Arutunian, *Arturo Ui*
☆ Freddy Wittop, *Hello, Dolly!*

CHOREOGRAPHER
☆ Gower Champion, *Hello, Dolly!*
Danny Daniels, *High Spirits*
Carol Haney, *Funny Girl*
Herbert Ross, *Anyone Can Whistle*

SPECIAL AWARD
☆ Eva Le Gallienne

1965

ACTOR (DRAMATIC)
John Gielgud, *Tiny Alice*
☆ Walter Matthau, *The Odd Couple*
Donald Pleasence, *Poor Bitos*
Jason Robards, *Hughie*

ACTRESS (DRAMATIC)
Marjorie Rhodes, *All In Good Time*
Bea Richards, *The Amen Corner*
Diana Sands, *The Owl and the Pussycat*
☆ Irene Worth, *Tiny Alice*

ACTOR, SUPPORTING OR FEATURED (DRAMATIC)
☆ Jack Albertson, *The Subject Was Roses*
Murray Hamilton, *Absence of a Cello*
Martin Sheen, *The Subject Was Roses*
Clarence Williams III, *Slow Dance on the Killing Ground*

ACTRESS, SUPPORTING OR FEATURED (DRAMATIC)
Rae Allen, *Traveller Without Luggage*
Alexandra Berlin, *All In Good Time*
Carolan Daniels, *Slow Dance on the Killing Ground*
☆ Alice Ghostley, *The Sign in Sidney Brustein's Window*

ACTOR (MUSICAL)
Sammy Davis, *Golden Boy*
☆ Zero Mostel, *Fiddler On The Roof*
Cyril Ritchard, *The Roar of the Greasepaint—The Smell of the Crowd*
Tommy Steele, *Half A Sixpence*

ACTRESS (MUSICAL)
Elizabeth Allen, *Do I Hear A Waltz?*
Nancy Dussault, *Bajour*
☆ Liza Minnelli, *Flora, the Red Menace*
Inga Swenson, *Baker Street*

ACTOR, SUPPORTING OR FEATURED (MUSICAL)
Jack Cassidy, *Fade Out—Fade In*
James Grout, *Half A Sixpence*
☆ Victor Spinetti, *Oh, What A Lovely War*
Jerry Orbach, *Guys and Dolls*

ACTRESS, SUPPORTING OR FEATURED (MUSICAL)
☆ Maria Karnilova, *Fiddler On The Roof*
Luba Lisa, *I Had A Ball*
Carrie Nye, *Half A Sixpence*
Barbara Windsor, *Oh, What A Lovely War*

PLAY
Luv by Murray Schisgal. Produced by Claire Nichtern
The Odd Couple by Neil Simon. Produced by Saint-Subber
☆ *The Subject Was Roses* by Frank Gilroy. Produced by Edgar
    Lansbury
Tiny Alice by Edward Albee. Produced by Theatre 1965, Richard
    Barr, and Clinton Wilder

AUTHOR (DRAMATIC)
Edward Albee, *Tiny Alice*
Frank Gilroy, *The Subject Was Roses*
Murray Schisgal, *Luv*
☆ Neil Simon, *The Odd Couple*

PRODUCER (DRAMATIC)
Hume Cronyn, Allen-Hogdon Inc., Stevens Productions Inc., and
    Bonfils-Seawell Enterprises, *Slow Dance on the Killing Ground*
☆ Claire Nichtern, *Luv*
Theatre 1965, Richard Barr, and Clinton Wilder, *Tiny Alice*
Robert Whitehead, *Tartuffe*

DIRECTOR (DRAMATIC)
William Ball, *Tartuffe*
Ulu Grosbard, *The Subject Was Roses*
☆ Mike Nichols, *Luv* and *The Odd Couple*
Alan Schneider, *Tiny Alice*

MUSICAL
☆ Fiddler On The Roof. Book by Joseph Stein, music by Jerry Bock, lyrics by Sheldon Harnick. Produced by Harold Prince

Golden Boy. Book by Clifford Odets and William Gibson, music by Charles Strouse, lyrics by Lee Adams. Produced by Hillard Elkins

Half A Sixpence. Book by Beverly Cross, music and lyrics by David Heneker. Produced by Allen Hodgdon, Stevens Productions, and Harold Fielding

Oh, What A Lovely War. Devised by Joan Littlewood for Theatre Workshop, Charles Chilton and Members of the Cast. Produced by David Merrick and Gerry Raffles

AUTHOR (MUSICAL)
Jerome Coopersmith, Baker Street
Beverly Cross, Half A Sixpence
Sidney Michaels, Ben Franklin In Paris
☆ Joseph Stein, Fiddler On The Roof

PRODUCER (MUSICAL)
Allen-Hodgdon, Stevens Productions and Harold Fielding, Half A Sixpence
Hillard Elkins, Golden Boy
David Merrick, The Roar of the Greasepaint—The Smell of the Crowd
☆ Harold Prince, Fiddler On The Roof

DIRECTOR (MUSICAL)
Joan Littlewood, Oh, What A Lovely War
Anthony Newley, The Roar of the Greasepaint—The Smell of the Crowd
☆ Jerome Robbins, Fiddler On The Roof
Gene Saks, Half A Sixpence

COMPOSER AND LYRICIST
☆ Jerry Bock and Sheldon Harnick, Fiddler On The Roof
Leslie Bricusse and Anthony Newley, The Roar of the Greasepaint—The Smell of the Crowd
David Heneker, Half A Sixpence
Richard Rodgers and Stephen Sondheim, Do I Hear A Waltz?

SCENIC DESIGNER
Boris Aronson, Fiddler On The Roof and Incident At Vichy
Sean Kenny, The Roar of the Greasepaint—The Smell of the Crowd
Beni Montresor, Do I Hear A Waltz?
☆ Oliver Smith, ☆ Baker Street, Luv and The Odd Couple

COSTUME DESIGNER
Jane Greenwood, *Tartuffe*
Motley, *Baker Street*
Freddy Wittop, *The Roar of the Greasepaint—The Smell of the Crowd*
☆ Patricia Zipprodt, *Fiddler On The Roof*

CHOREOGRAPHER
Peter Gennaro, *Bajour*
Donald McKayle, *Golden Boy*
☆ Jerome Robbins, *Fiddler On The Roof*
Onna White, *Half A Sixpence*

SPECIAL AWARDS
☆ Gilbert Miller
☆ Oliver Smith

1966

ACTOR (DRAMATIC)
Roland Culver, *Ivanov*
Donal Donnelly and Patrick Bedford, *Philadelphia, Here I Come!*
☆ Hal Holbrook, *Mark Twain Tonight!*
Nicol Williamson, *Inadmissible Evidence*

ACTRESS (DRAMATIC)
Sheila Hancock, *Entertaining Mr. Sloan*
☆ Rosemary Harris, *The Lion in Winter*
Kate Reid, *Slapstick Tragedy*
Lee Remick, *Wait Until Dark*

ACTOR, SUPPORTING OR FEATURED (DRAMATIC)
Burt Brinckerhoff, *Cactus Flower*
A. Larry Haines, *Generation*
Eamon Kelly, *Philadelphia, Here I Come!*
☆ Patrick Magee, *Marat/Sade*

ACTRESS, SUPPORTING OR FEATURED (DRAMATIC)
☆ Zoe Caldwell, *Slapstick Tragedy*
Glenda Jackson, *Marat/Sade*
Mairin D. O'Sullivan, *Philadelphia, Here I Come!*
Brenda Vaccaro, *Cactus Flower*

ACTOR (MUSICAL)
Jack Cassidy, *Superman*
John Cullum, *On A Clear Day You Can See Forever*

☆ Richard Kiley, *Man of La Mancha*
Harry Secombe, *Pickwick*

ACTRESS (MUSICAL)
Barbara Harris, *On A Clear Day*
Julie Harris, *Skyscraper*
☆ Angela Lansbury, *Mame*
Gwen Verdon, *Sweet Charity*

ACTOR, SUPPORTING OR FEATURED (MUSICAL)
Roy Castle, *Pickwick*
John McMartin, *Sweet Charity*
☆ Frankie Michaels, *Mame*
Michael O'Sullivan, *Superman*

ACTRESS, SUPPORTING OR FEATURED (MUSICAL)
☆ Beatrice Arthur, *Mame*
Helen Gallagher, *Sweet Charity*
Patricia Marand, *Superman*
Charlotte Rae, *Pickwick*

PLAY
Inadmissible Evidence by John Osborne. Produced by the David
    Merrick Arts Foundation
☆ *Marat/Sade* by Peter Weiss. English version by Geoffrey
    Skelton. Produced by the David Merrick Arts Foundation
Philadelphia, Here I Come! by Brian Friel. Produced by the David
    Merrick Arts Foundation
The Right Honourable Gentleman by Michael Dyne. Produced by
    Peter Cookson, Amy Lynn, and Walter Schwimmer

DIRECTOR (DRAMATIC)
☆ Peter Brook, *Marat/Sade*
Hilton Edwards, *Philadelphia, Here I Come!*
Ellis Rabb, *You Can't Take It With You*
Noel Willman, *The Lion in Winter*

MUSICAL
Mame. Book by Jerome Lawrence and Robert E. Lee, music and
    lyrics by Jerry Herman. Produced by Sylvia and Joseph
    Harris, Robert Fryer, and Lawrence Carr
☆ *Man of La Mancha.* Book by Dale Wasserman, music by Mitch
    Leigh, lyrics by Joe Darion. Produced by Albert W. Selden
    and Hal James
Skyscraper. Book by Peter Stone, music by James Van Heusen,
    lyrics by Sammy Cahn. Produced by Cy Feuer and Ernest M.
    Martin

Sweet Charity. Book by Neil Simon, music by Cy Coleman, lyrics by Dorothy Fields. Produced by Sylvia and Joseph Harris, Robert Fryer, and Lawrence Carr

DIRECTOR (MUSICAL)
Cy Feuer, *Skyscraper*
Bob Fosse, *Sweet Charity*
☆ Albert Marre, *Man of La Mancha*
Gene Saks, *Mame*

COMPOSER AND LYRICIST
Cy Coleman and Dorothy Fields, *Sweet Charity*
Jerry Herman, *Mame*
☆ Mitch Leigh and Joe Darion, *Man of La Mancha*
Burton Lane and Alan Jay Lerner, *On A Clear Day*

SCENIC DESIGNER
☆ Howard Bay, *Man of La Mancha*
William and Jean Eckart, *Mame*
David Hays, *Drat! The Cat!*
Robert Randolph, *Anya, Skyscraper,* and *Sweet Charity*

COSTUME DESIGNER
Loudon Sainthill, *The Right Honourable Gentleman*
Howard Bay and Patton Campbell, *Man of La Mancha*
Irene Sharaff, *Sweet Charity*
☆ Gunilla Palmstierna-Weiss, *Marat/Sade*

CHOREOGRAPHER
Jack Cole, *Man of La Mancha*
☆ Bob Fosse, *Sweet Charity*
Michael Kidd, *Skyscraper*
Onna White, *Mame*

SPECIAL AWARD
☆ Helen Menken (posthumous)

1967

ACTOR (DRAMATIC)
Hume Cronyn, *A Delicate Balance*
Donald Madden, *Black Comedy*
Donald Moffat, *Right You Are* and *The Wild Duck*
☆ Paul Rogers, *The Homecoming*

ACTRESS (DRAMATIC)
Eileen Atkins, *The Killing of Sister George*
Vivien Merchant, *The Homecoming*
Rosemary Murphy, *A Delicate Balance*
☆ Beryl Reid, *The Killing of Sister George*

ACTOR, SUPPORTING OR FEATURED (DRAMATIC)
Clayton Corzatte, *The School for Scandal*
Stephen Elliott, *Marat/Sade*
☆ Ian Holm, *The Homecoming*
Sydney Walker, *The Wild Duck*

ACTRESS, SUPPORTING OR FEATURED (DRAMATIC)
Camila Ashland, *Black Comedy*
Brenda Forbes, *The Loves of Cass McGuire*
☆ Marian Seldes, *A Delicate Balance*
Maria Tucci, *The Rose Tattoo*

ACTOR (MUSICAL)
Alan Alda, *The Apple Tree*
Jack Gilford, *Cabaret*
☆ Robert Preston, *I Do! I Do!*
Norman Wisdom, *Walking Happy*

ACTRESS (MUSICAL)
☆ Barbara Harris, *The Apple Tree*
Lotte Lenya, *Cabaret*
Mary Martin, *I Do! I Do!*
Louise Troy, *Walking Happy*

ACTOR, SUPPORTING OR FEATURED (MUSICAL)
Leon Bibb, *A Hand is on the Gate*
Gordon Dilworth, *Walking Happy*
☆ Joel Grey, *Cabaret*
Edward Winter, *Cabaret*

ACTRESS, SUPPORTING OR FEATURED (MUSICAL)
☆ Peg Murray, *Cabaret*
Leland Palmer, *A Joyful Noise*
Josephine Premice, *A Hand is on the Gate*
Susan Watson, *A Joyful Noise*

PLAY
A Delicate Balance by Edward Albee. Produced by Theatre 1967, Richard Barr, and Clinton Wilder
Black Comedy by Peter Shaffer. Produced by Alexander H. Cohen

☆ *The Homecoming* by Harold Pinter. Produced by Alexander H. Cohen

The Killing of Sister George by Frank Marcus. Produced by Helen Bonfils and Morton Gottlieb

DIRECTOR (DRAMATIC)
John Dexter, *Black Comedy*
Donald Driver, *Marat/Sade*
☆ Peter Hall, *The Homecoming*
Alan Schneider, *A Delicate Balance*

MUSICAL
☆ *Cabaret.* Book by Joe Masteroff, music by John Kander, lyrics by Fred Ebb. Produced by Harold Prince in association with Ruth Mitchell

I Do! I Do! Book and lyrics by Tom Jones, music by Harvey Schmidt. Produced by David Merrick

The Apple Tree. Book by Sheldon Harnick and Jerry Bock, music by Jerry Bock, lyrics by Sheldon Harnick. Produced by Stuart Ostrow

Walking Happy. Book by Roger O. Hirson and Ketti Frings, music by James Van Heusen, lyrics by Sammy Cahn. Produced by Cy Feuer and Ernest M. Martin

DIRECTOR (MUSICAL)
Gower Champion, *I Do! I Do!*
Mike Nichols, *The Apple Tree*
Jack Sydow, *Annie Get Your Gun*
☆ Harold Prince, *Cabaret*

COMPOSER AND LYRICIST
Jerry Bock and Sheldon Harnick, *The Apple Tree*
Sammy Cahn and James Van Heusen, *Walking Happy*
Tom Jones and Harvey Schmidt, *I Do! I Do!*
☆ John Kander and Fred Ebb, *Cabaret*

SCENE DESIGNER
☆ Boris Aronson, *Cabaret*
John Bury, *The Homecoming*
Oliver Smith, *I Do! I Do!*
Alan Tagg, *Black Comedy*

CHOREOGRAPHER
Michael Bennett, *A Joyful Noise*
Danny Daniels, *Walking Happy* and *Annie Get Your Gun*
☆ Ron Field, *Cabaret*
Lee Theodore, *The Apple Tree*

COSTUME DESIGNER

Nancy Potts, *The Wild Duck* and *The School for Scandal*
Tony Walton, *The Apple Tree*
Freddy Wittop, *I Do! I Do!*
☆ Patricia Zipprodt, *Cabaret*

1968

ACTOR (DRAMATIC)

☆ Martin Balsam, *You Know I Can't Hear You When the Water's Running*
Albert Finney, *Joe Egg*
Milo O'Shea, *Staircase*
Alan Webb, *I Never Sang for My Father*

ACTRESS (DRAMATIC)

☆ Zoe Caldwell, *The Prime of Miss Jean Brodie*
Colleen Dewhurst, *More Stately Mansions*
Maureen Stapleton, *Plaza Suite*
Dorothy Tutin, *Portrait of a Queen*

ACTOR, SUPPORTING OR FEATURED (DRAMATIC)

Paul Hecht, *Rosencrantz and Guildenstern Are Dead*
Brian Murray, *Rosencrantz and Guildenstern Are Dead*
☆ James Patterson, *The Birthday Party*
John Wood, *Rosencrantz and Guildenstern Are Dead*

ACTRESS, SUPPORTING OR FEATURED (DRAMATIC)

Pert Kelton, *Spofford*
☆ Zena Walker, *Joe Egg*
Ruth White, *The Birthday Party*
Eleanor Wilson, *Weekend*

ACTOR (MUSICAL)

☆ Robert Goulet, *The Happy Time*
Robert Hooks, *Hallelujah, Baby!*
Anthony Roberts, *How Now, Dow Jones*
David Wayne, *The Happy Time*

ACTRESS (MUSICAL)

Melina Mercouri, *Illya Darling*
☆ Patricia Routledge, *Darling of the Day*
☆ Leslie Uggams, *Hallelujah, Baby!*
Brenda Vaccaro, *How Now, Dow Jones*

ACTOR, SUPPORTING OR FEATURED (MUSICAL)
Scott Jacoby, *Golden Rainbow*
Nikos Kourkoulos, *Illya Darling*
Mike Rupert, *The Happy Time*
☆ Hiram Sherman, *How Now, Dow Jones*

ACTRESS, SUPPORTING OR FEATURED (MUSICAL)
Geula Gill, *The Grand Music Hall of Israel*
Julie Gregg, *The Happy Time*
☆ Lillian Hayman, *Hallelujah, Baby!*
Alice Playten, *Henry, Sweet Henry*

PLAY
Joe Egg by Peter Nichols. Produced by Joseph Cates and Henry
    Fownes
Plaza Suite by Neil Simon. Produced by Saint-Subber
☆ *Rosencrantz and Guildenstern Are Dead* by Tom Stoppard.
    Produced by The David Merrick Arts Foundation
The Price by Arthur Miller. Produced by Robert Whitehead

PRODUCER (DRAMATIC)
☆ David Merrick Arts Foundation, *Rosencrantz and Guildenstern Are*
    Dead

DIRECTOR (DRAMATIC)
Michael Blakemore, *Joe Egg*
Derek Goldby, *Rosencrantz and Guildenstern Are Dead*
☆ Mike Nichols, *Plaza Suite*
Alan Schneider, *You Know I Can't Hear You When the Water's Running*

MUSICAL
☆ *Hallelujah, Baby!* Book by Arthur Laurents, music by Jule Styne,
    lyrics by Betty Comden and Adolph Green. Produced by
    Albert Selden, Hal James, Jane C. Nusbaum, and Harry Rigby
The Happy Time. Book by N. Richard Nash, music by John Kander,
    lyrics by Fred Ebb. Produced by David Merrick
How Now, Dow Jones. Book by Max Shulman, music by Elmer Bern-
    stein, lyrics by Carolyn Leigh. Produced by David Merrick
Illya, Darling. Book by Jules Dassin, music by Manos Hadjidakis,
    lyrics by Joe Darion. Produced by Kermit Bloomgarden

PRODUCER (MUSICAL)
☆ Albert Selden, Hal James, Jane C. Nusbaum, and Harry Rigby,
    Hallelujah, Baby!

DIRECTOR (MUSICAL)
George Abbott, *How Now, Dow Jones*

☆ Gower Champion, *The Happy Time*
Jules Dassin, *Illya, Darling*
Burt Shevelove, *Hallelujah, Baby!*

COMPOSER AND LYRICIST
Elmer Bernstein and Carolyn Leigh, *How Now, Dow Jones*
Manos Hadjidakis and Joe Darion, *Illya Darling*
John Kander and Fred Ebb, *The Happy Time*
☆ Jule Styne, Betty Comden, and Adolph Green, *Hallelujah, Baby!*

SCENIC DESIGNER
Boris Aronson, *The Price*
☆ Desmond Heeley, *Rosencrantz and Guildenstern Are Dead*
Robert Randolph, *Golden Rainbow*
Peter Wexler, *The Happy Time*

COSTUME DESIGNER
Jane Greenwood, *More Stately Mansions*
☆ Desmond Heeley, *Rosencrantz and Guildenstern Are Dead*
Irene Sharaff, *Hallelujah, Baby!*
Freddy Wittop, *The Happy Time*

CHOREOGRAPHER
Michael Bennett, *Henry, Sweet Henry*
Kevin Carlisle, *Hallelujah, Baby!*
☆ Gower Champion, *The Happy Time*
Onna White, *Illya Darling*

SPECIAL AWARDS
☆ Audrey Hepburn
☆ Carol Channing
☆ Pearl Bailey
☆ David Merrick
☆ Maurice Chevalier
☆ APA-Phoenix Theatre
☆ Marlene Dietrich

1969

ACTOR (DRAMATIC)
Art Carney, *Lovers*
☆ James Earl Jones, *The Great White Hope*
Alec McCowen, *Hadrian VII*
Donald Pleasence, *The Man in the Glass Booth*

ACTRESS (DRAMATIC)

☆ Julie Harris, *Forty Carats*
Estelle Parsons, *Seven Descents of Myrtle*
Charlotte Rae, *Morning, Noon and Night*
Brenda Vaccaro, *The Goodbye People*

ACTOR, SUPPORTING OR FEATURED (DRAMATIC)

☆ Al Pacino, *Does a Tiger Wear a Necktie?*
Richard Castellano, *Lovers and Other Strangers*
Anthony Roberts, *Play It Again Sam*
Louis Zorich, *Hadrian* VII

ACTRESS, SUPPORTING OR FEATURED (DRAMATIC)

☆ Jane Alexander, *The Great White Hope*
Diane Keaton, *Play It Again Sam*
Lauren Jones, *Does a Tiger Wear a Necktie?*
Anna Manahan, *Lovers*

ACTOR (MUSICAL)

Herschel Bernardi, *Zorba*
Jack Cassidy, *Maggie Flynn*
Joel Grey, *George* M!
☆ Jerry Orbach, *Promises, Promises*

ACTRESS (MUSICAL)

Maria Karnilova, *Zorba*
☆ Angela Lansbury, *Dear World*
Dorothy Loudon, *The Fig Leaves Are Falling*
Jill O'Hara, *Promises, Promises*

ACTOR, SUPPORTING OR FEATURED (MUSICAL)

A. Larry Haines, *Promises, Promises*
☆ Ronald Holgate, *1776*
Edward Winter, *Promises, Promises*

ACTRESS, SUPPORTING OR FEATURED (MUSICAL)

Sandy Duncan, *Canterbury Tales*
☆ Marian Mercer, *Promises, Promises*
Lorraine Serabian, *Zorba*
Virginia Vestoff, *1776*

PLAY

☆ *The Great White Hope* by Howard Sackler. Produced by Herman
   Levin
Hadrian VII, by Peter Luke. Produced by Lester Osterman
   Productions, Bill Freedman, and Charles Kasher

Lovers by Brian Friel. Produced by Helen Bonfils and Morton Gottlieb

The Man in the Glass Booth by Robert Shaw. Produced by Glasshouse Productions and Peter Bridge, Ivor David Balding & Associates Ltd., and Edward M. Meyers with Leslie Ogden

DIRECTOR (DRAMATIC)

☆ Peter Dews, *Hadrian VII*
Joseph Hardy, *Play It Again Sam*
Harold Pinter, *The Man in the Glass Booth*
Michael A. Schultz, *Does a Tiger Wear a Necktie?*

MUSICAL

Hair. Book by Gerome Ragni and James Rado, music by Galt MacDermot, lyrics by James Rado. Produced by Michael Butler

Promises, Promises. Book by Neil Simon, music and lyrics by Burt Bacharach. Produced by David Merrick

☆ *1776*. Book by Peter Stone, music and lyrics by Sherman Edwards. Produced by Stuart Ostrow

Zorba. Book by Joseph Stein, music by John Kander, lyrics by Fred Ebb. Produced by Harold Prince

DIRECTOR (MUSICAL)

☆ Peter Hunt, *1776*
Robert Moore, *Promises, Promises*
Tom O'Horgan, *Hair*
Harold Prince, *Zorba*

SCENIC DESIGNER

☆ Boris Aronson, *Zorba*
Derek Cousins, *Canterbury Tales*
Jo Mielziner, *1776*
Oliver Smith, *Dear World*

COSTUME DESIGNER

Michael Annals, *Morning, Noon and Night*
Robert Fletcher, *Hadrian VII*
☆ Louden Sainthill, *Canterbury Tales*
Patricia Zipprodt, *Zorba*

CHOREOGRAPHER

Sammy Bayes, *Canterbury Tales*
Ronald Field, *Zorba*
☆ Joe Layton, *George M!*
Michael Bennett, *Promises, Promises*

SPECIAL AWARDS
☆ The National Theatre Company of Great Britain
☆ The Negro Ensemble Company
☆ Rex Harrison
☆ Leonard Bernstein
☆ Carol Burnett

The 1970s

"Lighting design as an art and craft in the theatre is one that receives little notice. And rightly so, because light itself is invisible and only enables you to see objects and humans that the light falls upon. For the majority of theatrical productions lighting is an unseen tool that guides the audience's eyes and aids in creating a mood and atmosphere. Thus when lighting is very good it is hardly noticed, and only on a subconscious level can you connect the quality of the lighting with the overall enjoyment and appreciation of the play. Thus for many years I have taken pride in the fact that when I had done my best work no one might notice and thus I could rationalize why I had never received any awards for my work.

Now that I have won a Tony® Award I must work even harder to make my work unseen and keep it a secret so that more people can enjoy the theatre."

Jules Fisher

1970

ACTOR (DRAMATIC)
James Coco, *Last of the Red Hot Lovers*
Frank Grimes, *Borstal Boy*
Stacy Keach, *Indians*
☆ Fritz Weaver, *Child's Play*

ACTRESS (DRAMATIC)
Geraldine Brooks, *Brightower*
☆ Tammy Grimes, *Private Lives* (Revival)
Helen Hayes, *Harvey* (Revival)

ACTOR, SUPPORTING OR FEATURED (DRAMATIC)
Joseph Bova, *The Chinese and Dr. Fish*
☆ Ken Howard, *Child's Play*
Dennis King, *A Patriot for Me*

ACTRESS, SUPPORTING OR FEATURED (DRAMATIC)
☆ Blythe Danner, *Butterflies Are Free*
Alice Drummond, *The Chinese and Dr. Fish*
Eileen Heckart, *Butterflies Are Free*
Linda Lavin, *Last of the Red Hot Lovers*

ACTOR (MUSICAL)
Len Cariou, *Applause*
☆ Cleavon Little, *Purlie*
Robert Weede, *Cry for Us All*

ACTRESS (MUSICAL)
☆ Lauren Bacall, *Applause*
Katharine Hepburn, *Coco*
Dilys Watling, *Georgy*

ACTOR, SUPPORTING OR FEATURED (MUSICAL)
☆ René Auberjonois, *Coco*
Brandon Maggart, *Applause*
George Rose, *Coco*

ACTRESS, SUPPORTING OR FEATURED (MUSICAL)
Bonnie Franklin, *Applause*
Penny Fuller, *Applause*
Melissa Hart, *Georgy*
☆ Melba Moore, *Purlie*

PLAY

☆ *Borstal Boy* by Frank McMahon. Produced by Michael McAloney and Burton C. Kaiser

Child's Play by Robert Marasco. Produced by David Merrick

Indians by Arthur Kopit. Produced by Lyn Austin, Oliver Smith, Joel Schenker, and Roger L. Stevens

Last of the Red Hot Lovers by Neil Simon. Produced by Saint-Subber

DIRECTOR (DRAMATIC)

☆ Joseph Hardy, *Child's Play*

Milton Katselas, *Butterflies Are Free*

Tomas MacAnna, *Borstal Boy*

Robert Moore, *Last of the Red Hot Lovers*

MUSICAL

☆ *Applause*. Book by Betty Comden and Adolph Green, music by Charles Strouse, lyrics by Lee Adams. Produced by Joseph Kipness and Lawrence Kasha

Coco. Book and lyrics by Alan Jay Lerner, music by André Previn. Produced by Frederick Brisson

Purlie. Book by Ossie Davis, Philip Rose, and Peter Udell, music by Gary Geld, lyrics by Peter Udell. Produced by Philip Rose

DIRECTOR (MUSICAL)

Michael Benthall, *Coco*

☆ Ron Field, *Applause*

Philip Rose, *Purlie*

SCENIC DESIGNER

Howard Bay, *Cry for Us All*

Ming Cho Lee, *Billy*

☆ Jo Mielziner, *Child's Play*

Robert Randolph, *Applause*

COSTUME DESIGNER

Ray Aghayan, *Applause*

☆ Cecil Beaton, *Coco*

W. Robert Lavine, *Jimmy*

Freddy Wittop, *A Patriot for Me*

CHOREOGRAPHER

Michael Bennett, *Coco*

Grover Dale, *Billy*

☆ Ron Field, *Applause*

Louis Johnson, *Purlie*

LIGHTING DESIGNER
☆ Jo Mielziner, *Child's Play*
Tharon Musser, *Applause*
Thomas Skelton, *Indians*

SPECIAL AWARDS
☆ Noel Coward
☆ Alfred Lunt and Lynn Fontanne
☆ New York Shakespeare Festival
☆ Barbra Streisand

1971

ACTOR (DRAMATIC)
☆ Brian Bedford, *The School for Wives*
John Gielgud, *Home*
Alec McCowen, *The Philanthropist*
Ralph Richardson, *Home*

ACTRESS (DRAMATIC)
Estelle Parsons, *And Miss Reardon Drinks a Little*
Diana Rigg, *Abelard and Heloise*
Marian Seldes, *Father's Day*
☆ Maureen Stapleton, *Gingerbread Lady*

ACTOR, SUPPORTING OR FEATURED (DRAMATIC)
Ronald Radd, *Abelard and Heloise*
Donald Pickering, *Conduct Unbecoming*
☆ Paul Sand, *Story Theatre*
Ed Zimmermann, *The Philanthropist*

ACTRESS, SUPPORTING OR FEATURED (DRAMATIC)
☆ Rae Allen, *And Miss Reardon Drinks a Little*
Lili Darvas, *Les Blancs*
Joan Van Ark, *The School for Wives*
Mona Washbourne, *Home*

ACTOR (MUSICAL)
David Burns, *Lovely Ladies, Kind Gentlemen*
Larry Kert, *Company*
☆ Hal Linden, *The Rothschilds*
Bobby Van, *No, No, Nanette* (Revival)

ACTRESS (MUSICAL)
Susan Browning, *Company*

Sandy Duncan, *The Boy Friend*
☆ Helen Gallagher, *No, No, Nanette*
Elaine Stritch, *Company*

ACTOR, SUPPORTING OR FEATURED (MUSICAL)
☆ Keene Curtis, *The Rothschilds*
Charles Kimbrough, *Company*
Walter Willison, *Two By Two*

ACTRESS, SUPPORTING OR FEATURED (MUSICAL)
Barbara Barrie, *Company*
☆ Patsy Kelly, *No, No, Nanette*
Pamela Myers, *Company*

PLAY
Home by David Storey. Produced by Alexander H. Cohen
☆ *Sleuth* by Anthony Shaffer. Produced by Helen Bonfils, Morton
    Gottlieb, and Michael White
Story Theatre by Paul Sills. Produced by Zev Bufman
The Philanthropist by Christopher Hampton. Produced by David
    Merrick and Byron Goldman

PRODUCER (DRAMATIC)
Alexander H. Cohen, *Home*
David Merrick, *The Philanthropist*
☆ Helen Bonfils, Morton Gottlieb, and Michael White, *Sleuth*
Zev Bufman, *Story Theatre*

DIRECTOR (DRAMATIC)
Lindsay Anderson, *Home*
☆ Peter Brook, *A Midsummer Night's Dream*
Stephen Porter, *The School for Wives*
Clifford Williams, *Sleuth*

MUSICAL
☆ *Company*. Produced by Harold Prince
The Me Nobody Knows. Produced by Jeff Britton
The Rothschilds. Produced by Lester Osterman and Hillard Elkins

PRODUCER (MUSICAL)
☆ Harold Prince, *Company*
Jeff Britton, *The Me Nobody Knows*
Hillard Elkins and Lester Osterman, *The Rothschilds*

DIRECTOR (MUSICAL)
Michael Kidd, *The Rothschilds*
Robert H. Livingston, *The Me Nobody Knows*

☆ Harold Prince, *Company*
Burt Shevelove, *No, No, Nanette*

BOOK (MUSICAL)
☆ George Furth, *Company*
Robert H. Livingston and Herb Schapiro, *The Me Nobody Knows*
Sherman Yellen, *The Rothschilds*

LYRICS (MUSICAL)
Sheldon Harnick, *The Rothschilds*
Will Holt, *The Me Nobody Knows*
☆ Stephen Sondheim, *Company*

SCORE (MUSICAL)
Jerry Bock, *The Rothschilds*
Gary William Friedman, *The Me Nobody Knows*
☆ Stephen Sondheim, *Company*

SCENIC DESIGNER
☆ Boris Aronson, *Company*
John Bury, *The Rothschilds*
Sally Jacobs, *A Midsummer Night's Dream*
Jo Mielziner, *Father's Day*

COSTUME DESIGNER
☆ Raoul Pène Du Bois, *No, No, Nanette*
Jane Greenwood, *Hay Fever* and *Les Blancs*
Freddy Wittop, *Lovely Ladies, Kind Gentlemen*

CHOREOGRAPHER
Michael Bennett, *Company*
Michael Kidd, *The Rothschilds*
☆ Donald Saddler, *No, No, Nanette*

LIGHTING DESIGNER
Robert Ornbo, *Company*
☆ H. R. Poindexter, *Story Theatre*
William Ritman, *Sleuth*

SPECIAL AWARDS
☆ Elliot Norton
☆ Ingram Ash
☆ Playbill
☆ Roger L. Stevens

1972

ACTOR (DRAMATIC)
Tom Aldredge, *Sticks and Bones*
Donald Pleasence, *Wise Child*
☆ Cliff Gorman, *Lenny*
Jason Robards, *The Country Girl*

ACTRESS (DRAMATIC)
Eileen Atkins, *Vivat! Vivat Regina!*
Colleen Dewhurst, *All Over*
Rosemary Harris, *Old Times*
☆ Sada Thompson, *Twigs*

ACTOR, SUPPORTING OR FEATURED (DRAMATIC)
☆ Vincent Gardenia, *The Prisoner of Second Avenue*
Douglas Rain, *Vivat! Vivat Regina!*
Lee Richardson, *Vivat! Vivat Regina!*
Joe Silver, *Lenny*

ACTRESS, SUPPORTING OR FEATURED (DRAMATIC)
Cara Duff-MacCormick, *Moonchildren*
Mercedes McCambridge, *The Love Suicide at Schofield Barracks*
Frances Sternhagen, *The Sign in Sidney Brustein's Window* (Revival)
☆ Elizabeth Wilson, *Sticks and Bones*

ACTOR (MUSICAL)
Clifton Davis, *Two Gentlemen of Verona*
Barry Bostwick, *Grease*
Raul Julia, *Two Gentlemen of Verona*
☆ Phil Silvers, *A Funny Thing Happened on the Way to the Forum*
(Revival)

ACTRESS (MUSICAL)
Jonelle Allen, *Two Gentlemen of Verona*
Dorothy Collins, *Follies*
Mildred Natwick, *70 Girls 70*
☆ Alexis Smith, *Follies*

ACTOR, SUPPORTING OR FEATURED (MUSICAL)
☆ Larry Blyden, *A Funny Thing Happened on the Way to the Forum*
(Revival)
Timothy Myers, *Grease*
Gene Nelson, *Follies*
Ben Vereen, *Jesus Christ Superstar*

ACTRESS, SUPPORTING OR FEATURED (MUSICAL)

Adrienne Barbeau, *Grease*

☆ Linda Hopkins, *Inner City*

Bernadette Peters, *On The Town* (Revival)

Beatrice Wind, *Ain't Supposed to Die a Natural Death*

PLAY

Old Times by Harold Pinter. Produced by Roger L. Stevens

The Prisoner of Second Avenue by Neil Simon. Produced by Saint-Subber

☆ *Sticks and Bones* by David Rabe. Produced by New York Shakespeare Festival–Joseph Papp

Vivat! Vivat Regina! by Robert Bolt. Produced by David Merrick and Arthur Cantor

DIRECTOR (DRAMATIC)

Jeff Bleckner, *Sticks and Bones*

Gordon Davidson, *The Trial Of The Catonsville Nine*

Peter Hall, *Old Times*

☆ Mike Nichols, *The Prisoner of Second Avenue*

MUSICAL

Ain't Supposed to Die a Natural Death. Produced by Eugene V. Wolsk, Charles Blackwell, Emanuel Azenberg, and Robert Malina

Follies. Produced by Harold Prince

☆ *Two Gentlemen of Verona*. Produced by New York Shakespeare Festival–Joseph Papp

Grease. Produced by Kenneth Waissman and Maxine Fox

DIRECTOR (MUSICAL)

Gilbert Moses, *Ain't Supposed to Die a Natural Death*

☆ Harold Prince and Michael Bennett, *Follies*

Mel Shapiro, *Two Gentlemen of Verona*

Burt Shevelove, *A Funny Thing Happened on the Way to the Forum*

BOOK (MUSICAL)

Ain't Supposed to Die a Natural Death by Melvin Van Peebles

Follies by James Goldman

Grease by Jim Jacobs and Warren Casey

☆ *Two Gentlemen of Verona* by John Guare and Mel Shapiro

SCORE

Ain't Supposed to Die a Natural Death. Music and lyrics by Melvin Van Peebles

☆ *Follies*. Music and lyrics by Stephen Sondheim

Jesus Christ Superstar. Music by Andrew Lloyd Webber, lyrics by Tim Rice

Two Gentlemen of Verona. Music by Galt MacDermot, lyrics by John Guare

SCENIC DESIGNER
☆ Boris Aronson, *Follies*
John Bury, *Old Times*
Kert Lundell, *Ain't Supposed to Die a Natural Death*
Robin Wagner, *Jesus Christ Superstar*

COSTUMER DESIGNER
Theoni V. Aldredge, *Two Gentlemen of Verona*
Randy Barcelo, *Jesus Christ Superstar*
☆ Florence Klotz, *Follies*
Carrie F. Robbins, *Grease*

CHOREOGRAPHER
☆ Michael Bennett, *Follies*
Patricia Birch, *Grease*
Jean Erdman, *Two Gentlemen of Verona*

LIGHTING DESIGNER
Martin Aronstein, *Ain't Supposed to Die a Natural Death*
John Bury, *Old Times*
Jules Fisher, *Jesus Christ Superstar*
☆ Tharon Musser, *Follies*

SPECIAL AWARDS
☆ The Theatre Guild-American Theatre Society
☆ Richard Rodgers
☆ *Fiddler on the Roof*
☆ Ethel Merman

1973

ACTOR (DRAMATIC)
Jack Albertson, *The Sunshine Boys*
☆ Alan Bates, *Butley*
Wilfrid Hyde White, *The Jockey Club Stakes*
Paul Sorvino, *That Championship Season*

ACTRESS (DRAMATIC)
Jane Alexander, *6 Rms Riv Vu*
Colleen Dewhurst, *Mourning Becomes Electra*
☆ Julie Harris, *The Last of Mrs. Lincoln*
Kathleen Widdoes, *Much Ado About Nothing*

Actor, Supporting or Featured (Dramatic)

Barnard Hughes, *Much Ado About Nothing*
☆ John Lithgow, *The Changing Room*
John McMartin, *Don Juan*
Hayward Morse, *Butley*

Actress, Supporting or Featured (Dramatic)

Maya Angelou, *Look Away*
☆ Leora Dana, *The Last of Mrs. Lincoln*
Katherine Helmond, *The Great God Brown*
Penelope Windust, *Elizabeth I*

Actor (Musical)

Len Cariou, *A Little Night Music*
Robert Morse, *Sugar*
Brock Peters, *Lost in the Stars*
☆ Ben Vereen, *Pippin*

Actress (Musical)

☆ Glynis Johns, *A Little Night Music*
Leland Palmer, *Pippin*
Debbie Reynolds, *Irene* (Revival)
Marcia Rodd, *Shelter*

Actor, Supporting or Featured (Musical)

Laurence Guittard, *A Little Night Music*
☆ George S. Irving, *Irene*
Avon Long, *Don't Play Us Cheap*
Gilbert Price, *Lost in the Stars*

Actress, Supporting or Featured (Musical)

☆ Patricia Elliot, *A Little Night Music*
Hermione Gingold, *A Little Night Music*
Patsy Kelly, *Irene*
Irene Ryan, *Pippin*

Play

Butley by Simon Gray. Produced by Lester Osterman and Richard Horner
☆ *That Championship Season* by Jason Miller. Produced by the New York Shakespeare Festival–Joseph Papp
The Changing Room by David Storey. Produced by Charles Bowden, Lee Reynolds, and Isobel Robins
The Sunshine Boys by Neil Simon. Produced by Emanuel Azenberg and Eugene V. Wolsk

DIRECTOR (DRAMATIC)
☆ A. J. Antoon, *That Championship Season*
A. J. Antoon, *Much Ado About Nothing*
Alan Arkin, *The Sunshine Boys*
Michael Rudman, *The Changing Room*

MUSICAL
☆ *A Little Night Music*. Produced by Harold Prince
Don't Bother Me, I Can't Cope. Produced by Edward Padula and Arch
    Lustberg
Pippin. Produced by Stuart Ostrow
Sugar. Produced by David Merrick

DIRECTOR (MUSICAL)
Vinnette Carroll, *Don't Bother Me, I Can't Cope*
Gower Champion, *Sugar*
☆ Bob Fosse, *Pippin*
Harold Prince, *A Little Night Music*

BOOK (MUSICAL)
☆ *A Little Night Music* by Hugh Wheeler
Don't Bother Me, I Can't Cope by Micki Grant
Don't Play Us Cheap by Melvin Van Peebles
Pippin by Roger O. Hirson

SCORE (MUSICAL)
☆ *A Little Night Music*. Music and lyrics by Stephen Sondheim
Don't Bother Me, I Can't Cope. Music and lyrics by Micki Grant
Much Ado About Nothing. Music by Peter Link
Pippin. Music and lyrics by Stephen Schwartz

SCENIC DESIGNER
Boris Aronson, *A Little Night Music*
David Jenkins, *The Changing Room*
Santo Loquasto, *That Championship Season*
☆ Tony Walton, *Pippin*

COSTUME DESIGNER
Theoni V. Aldredge, *Much Ado About Nothing*
☆ Florence Klotz, *A Little Night Music*
Miles White, *Tricks*
Patricia Zipprodt, *Pippin*

CHOREOGRAPHER
Gower Champion, *Sugar*
☆ Bob Fosse, *Pippin*

Peter Gennaro, *Irene*
Donald Saddler, *Much Ado About Nothing*

LIGHTING DESIGNER
Martin Aronstein, *Much Ado About Nothing*
Ian Calderon, *That Championship Season*
☆ Jules Fisher, *Pippin*
Tharon Musser, *A Little Night Music*

SPECIAL AWARDS
☆ John Lindsay
☆ Actors' Fund of America
☆ Shubert Organization

1974

ACTOR (DRAMATIC)
☆ Michael Moriarty, *Find Your Way Home*
Zero Mostel, *Ulysses in Nighttown*
Jason Robards, *A Moon for the Misbegotten* (Revival)
George C. Scott, *Vanya* (Revival)
Nicol Williamson, *Uncle Vanya*

ACTRESS (DRAMATIC)
Jane Alexander, *Find Your Way Home*
☆ Colleen Dewhurst, *A Moon for the Misbegotten*
Julie Harris, *The Au Pair Man*
Madeline Kahn, *Boom Boom Room*
Rachel Roberts, performances with the *New Phoenix Repertory Company*

ACTOR, SUPPORTING OR FEATURED (DRAMATIC)
René Auberjonois, *The Good Doctor*
☆ Ed Flanders, *A Moon for the Misbegotten*
Douglas Turner Ward, *The River Niger*
Dick Anthony Williams, *What the Wine-Sellers Buy*

ACTRESS, SUPPORTING OR FEATURED (DRAMATIC)
Regina Baff, *Veronica's Room*
Fionnula Flanagan, *Ulysses in Nighttown*
Charlotte Moore, *Chemin de Fer*
Roxie Roker, *The River Niger*
☆ Frances Sternhagen, *The Good Doctor*

ACTOR (MUSICAL)
Alfred Drake, *Gigi*

Joe Morton, *Raisin*
☆ Christopher Plummer, *Cyrano*
Lewis J. Stadlen, *Candide*

ACTRESS (MUSICAL)
☆ Virginia Capers, *Raisin*
Carol Channing, *Lorelei*
Michele Lee, *Seesaw*

ACTOR, SUPPORTING OR FEATURED (MUSICAL)
Mark Baker, *Candide*
Ralph Carter, *Raisin*
☆ Tommy Tune, *Seesaw*

ACTRESS, SUPPORTING OR FEATURED (MUSICAL)
Leigh Berry, *Cyrano*
Maureen Brennan, *Candide*
June Gable, *Candide*
Ernestine Jackson, *Raisin*
☆ Janie Sell, *Over Here!*

PLAY
Boom Boom Room by David Rabe. Produced by Joseph Papp
The Au Pair Man by Hugh Leonard. Produced by Joseph Papp
☆ *The River Niger* by Joseph A. Walker. Produced by Negro
    Ensemble Co., Inc.
Ulysses in Nighttown by Marjorie Barkentin. Produced by Alexander
    H. Cohen and Bernard Delfont

DIRECTOR (DRAMATIC)
Burgess Meredith, *Ulysses in Nighttown*
Mike Nichols, *Uncle Vanya*
Stephen Porter, *Chemin de Fer*
☆ José Quintero, *A Moon for the Misbegotten*
Edwin Sherin, *Find Your Way Home*

MUSICAL
Over Here! Produced by Kenneth Waissman and Maxine Fox
☆ *Raisin*. Produced by Robert Nemiroff
Seesaw. Produced by Joseph Kipness, Lawrence Kasha, James
    Nederlander, George M. Steinbrenner III, and Lorin E. Price

DIRECTOR (MUSICAL)
Michael Bennett, *Seesaw*
Donald McKayle, *Raisin*
☆ Harold Prince, *Candide*
Tom Moore, *Over Here!*

BOOK (MUSICAL)
☆ *Candide* by Hugh Wheeler
Raisin by Robert Nemiroff and Charlotte Zaltzberg
Seesaw by Michael Bennett

SCORE
☆ *Gigi*. Music by Frederick Loewe, lyrics by Alan Jay Lerner
The Good Doctor. Music by Peter Link, lyrics by Neil Simon
Raisin. Music by Judd Woldin, lyrics by Robert Brittan
Seesaw. Music by Cy Coleman, lyrics by Dorothy Fields

SCENIC DESIGNER
John Conklin, *The Au Pair Man*
☆ Franne and Eugene Lee, *Candide*
Santo Loquasto, *What the Wine-Sellers Buy*
Oliver Smith, *Gigi*
Ed Wittstein, *Ulysses in Nighttown*

COSTUME DESIGNER
Theoni V. Aldredge, *The Au Pair Man*
Finlay James, *Crown Matrimonial*
☆ Franne Lee, *Candide*
Oliver Messel, *Gigi*
Carrie F. Robbins, *Over Here!*

CHOREOGRAPHER
☆ Michael Bennett, *Seasaw*
Patricia Birch, *Over Here!*
Donald McKayle, *Raisin*

LIGHTING DESIGNER
Martin Aronstein, *Boom Boom Room*
Ken Billington, *The Visit* (Revival)
Ben Edwards, *A Moon for the Misbegotten*
☆ Jules Fisher, *Ulysses in Nighttown*
Tharon Musser, *The Good Doctor*

SPECIAL AWARDS
☆ Liza Minnelli
☆ Bette Midler
☆ Peter Cook and Dudley Moore, *Good Evening*
A Moon for the Misbegotten
Candide
☆ Actors' Equity Association
☆ Theatre Development Fund
☆ John F. Wharton
☆ Harold Friedlander

1975

ACTOR (DRAMATIC)
James Dale, *Scapino*
Peter Firth, *Equus*
Henry Fonda, *Clarence Darrow*
Ben Gazzara, *Hughie and Duet*
☆ John Kani and Winston Ntshona, *Sizwe Banzi is Dead and The Island*
John Wood, *Sherlock Holmes*

ACTRESS (DRAMATIC)
Elizabeth Ashley, *Cat on a Hot Tin Roof*
☆ Ellen Burstyn, *Same Time, Next Year*
Diana Rigg, *The Misanthrope*
Maggie Smith, *Private Lives*
Liv Ullmann, *A Doll's House*

ACTOR, SUPPORTING OR FEATURED (DRAMATIC)
Larry Blyden, *Absurd Person Singular*
Leonard Frey, *The National Health*
☆ Frank Langella, *Seascape*
Philip Locke, *Sherlock Holmes*
George Rose, *My Fat Friend*
Dick Anthony Williams, *Black Picture Show*

ACTRESS, SUPPORTING OR FEATURED (DRAMATIC)
Linda Miller, *Black Picture Show*
☆ Rita Moreno, *The Ritz*
Geraldine Page, *Absurd Person Singular*
Carole Shelley, *Absurd Person Singular*
Elizabeth Spriggs, *London Assurance*
Frances Sternhagen, *Equus*

ACTOR (MUSICAL)
☆ John Cullum, *Shenandoah*
Joel Grey, *Goodtime Charley*
Raul Julia, *Where's Charley?*
Eddie Mekka, *The Lieutenant*
Robert Preston, *Mack and Mabel*

ACTRESS (MUSICAL)
Lola Falana, *Doctor Jazz*
☆ Angela Lansbury, *Gypsy*

Bernadette Peters, *Mack and Mabel*
Ann Reinking, *Goodtime Charley*

ACTOR, SUPPORTING OR FEATURED (MUSICAL)
Tom Aldredge, *Where's Charley?*
John Bottoms, *Dance with Me*
Douglas Henning, *The Magic Show*
Gilbert Price, *The Night That Made America Famous*
☆ Ted Ross, *The Wiz*
Richard B. Shull, *Goodtime Charley*

ACTRESS, SUPPORTING OR FEATURED (MUSICAL)
☆ Dee Dee Bridgewater, *The Wiz*
Susan Browning, *Goodtime Charley*
Zan Charisse, *Gypsy*
Taina Elg, *Where's Charley?*
Kelly Garrett, *The Night That Made America Famous*
Donna Theodore, *Shenandoah*

PLAY
☆ *Equus* by Peter Shaffer. Produced by Kermit Bloomgarden and
    Doris Cole Abrahams
Same Time, Next Year by Bernard Slade. Produced by Morton
    Gottlieb
Seascape by Edward Albee. Produced by Richard Barr, Charles
    Woodward, and Clinton Wilder
Short Eyes by Miguel Pinero. Produced by Joseph Papp, New York
    Shakespeare Festival
Sizwe Banzi is Dead and The Island by Athol Fugard, John Kani, and
    Winston Ntshona. Produced by Hillard Elkins, Lester
    Osterman Productions, Bernard Delfont, and Michael White
The National Health by Peter Nichols. Produced by Circle in the
    Square, Inc.

DIRECTOR (DRAMATIC)
Arvin Brown, *The National Health*
☆ John Dexter, *Equus*
Frank Dunlop, *Scapino*
Ronald Eyre, *London Assurance*
Athol Fugard, *Sizwe Banzi is Dead and The Island*
Gene Saks, *Same Time, Next Year*

MUSICAL
Mack and Mabel. Produced by David Merrick

The Lieutenant. Produced by Joseph Kutrzeba and Spofford Beadle
Shenandoah. Produced by Philip Rose, and Gloria and Louis K. Sher
☆ *The Wiz.* Produced by Ken Harper

DIRECTOR (MUSICAL)
Gower Champion, *Mack and Mabel*
Grover Dale, *The Magic Show*
☆ Geoffrey Holder, *The Wiz*
Arthur Laurents, *Gypsy*

BOOK (MUSICAL)
Mack and Mabel by Michael Stewart
☆ *Shenandoah* by James Lee Barrett, Peter Udell, and Philip Rose
The Lieutenant by Gene Curty, Nitra Scharfman, and Chuck Strand
The Wiz by William F. Brown

SCORE
Letter for Queen Victoria. Music and lyrics by Alan Lloyd
Shenandoah. Music by Gary Geld, lyrics by Peter Udell
The Lieutenant. Music and lyrics by Gene Curty, Nitra Scharfman, and Chuck Strand
☆ *The Wiz.* Music and lyrics by Charlie Smalls

SCENIC DESIGNER
Scott Johnson, *Dance With Me*
Tanya Moiseiwitsch, *The Misanthrope*
William Ritman, *God's Favorite*
Rouben Ter-Arutunian, *Goodtime Charley*
☆ Carl Toms, *Sherlock Holmes*
Robert Wagner, *Mack and Mabel*

COSTUME DESIGNER
Arthur Boccia, *Where's Charley*
Raoul Pène du Bois, *Doctor Jazz*
☆ Geoffrey Holder, *The Wiz*
Willa Kim, *Goodtime Charley*
Tanya Moiseiwitsch, *The Misanthrope*
Patricia Zipprodt, *Mack and Mabel*

CHOREOGRAPHER
Gower Champion, *Mack and Mabel*
☆ George Faison, *The Wiz*
Donald McKayle, *Doctor Jazz*
Margo Sappington, *Where's Charley?*

Robert Tucker, *Shenandoah*
Joel Zwick, *Dance with Me*

Lighting Designer
Chip Monk, *The Rocky Horror Show*
Abe Feder, *Goodtime Charley*
☆ Neil Peter Jampolis, *Sherlock Holmes*
Andy Phillips, *Equus*
Thomas Skelton, *All God's Chillun*
James Tilton, *Seascape*

Special Awards
☆ Neil Simon
☆ Al Hirschfeld

1976

Actor (Play)
Moses Gunn, *The Poison Tree*
George C. Scott, *Death of a Salesman*
Donald Sinden, *Habeas Corpus*
☆ John Wood, *Travesties*

Actress (Play)
Tovah Feldshuh, *Yentl*
Rosemary Harris, *The Royal Family*
Lynn Redgrave, *Mrs. Warren's Profession*
☆ Irene Worth, *Sweet Bird of Youth*

Actor (Featured Role—Play)
Barry Bostwick, *They Knew What They Wanted*
Gabriel Dell, *Lamppost Reunion*
☆ Edward Herrmann, *Mrs. Warren's Profession*
Daniel Seltzer, *Knock Knock*

Actress (Featured Role—Play)
Mary Beth Hurt, *Trelawny of the 'Wells'*
☆ Shirley Knight, *Kennedy's Children*
Lois Nettleton, *They Knew What They Wanted*
Meryl Streep, *27 Wagons Full of Cotton*

Actor (Musical)
Mako, *Pacific Overtures*
Jerry Orbach, *Chicago*
Ian Richardson, *My Fair Lady*
☆ George Rose, *My Fair Lady*

ACTRESS (MUSICAL)
☆ Donna McKechnie, A *Chorus Line*
Vivian Reed, *Bubbling Brown Sugar*
Chita Rivera, *Chicago*
Gwen Verdon, *Chicago*

ACTOR (FEATURED ROLE—MUSICAL)
Robert LuPone, A *Chorus Line*
Charles Repole, *Very Good Eddie*
Isao Sato, *Pacific Overtures*
☆ Sammy Williams, A *Chorus Line*

ACTRESS (FEATURED ROLE—MUSICAL)
☆ Carole Bishop, A *Chorus Line*
Priscilla Lopez, A *Chorus Line*
Patti LuPone, *The Robber Bridegroom*
Virginia Seidel, *Very Good Eddie*

PLAY
The First Breeze of Summer by Leslie Lee. Produced by Negro
    Ensemble Co., Inc.
Knock Knock by Jules Feiffer. Produced by Harry Rigby and Terry
    Allen Kramer
Lamppost Reunion by Louis LaRusso II. Produced by Joe Garofalo
☆ *Travesties* by Tom Stoppard. Produced by David Merrick, Doris
    Cole Abrahams, and Burry Fredrik in association with S.
    Spencer Davids and Eddie Kulukundis

DIRECTOR (PLAY)
Arvin Brown, *Ah Wilderness*
Marshall W. Mason, *Knock Knock*
☆ Ellis Rabb, *The Royal Family*
Peter Wood, *Travesties*

MUSICAL
☆ A *Chorus Line*. Produced by Joseph Papp, New York
    Shakespeare Festival
Bubbling Brown Sugar. Produced by J. Lloyd Grant, Richard Bell,
    Robert M. Cooper, and Ashton Springer in association with
    Moe Septee, Inc.
Chicago. Produced by Robert Fryer and James Cresson
Pacific Overtures. Produced by Harold Prince in association with
    Ruth Mitchell

DIRECTOR (MUSICAL)
☆ Michael Bennett, A *Chorus Line*

Bob Fosse, *Chicago*
Bill Gile, *Very Good Eddie*
Harold Prince, *Pacific Overtures*

Book (Musical)
☆ A *Chorus Line* by James Kirkwood and Nicholas Dante
Chicago by Fred Ebb and Bob Fosse
Pacific Overtures by John Weidman
The Robber Bridegroom by Alfred Uhry

Score
☆ A *Chorus Line*. Music by Marvin Hamlisch, lyrics by Edward Kleban
Chicago. Music by John Kander, lyrics by Fred Ebb
Pacific Overtures. Music and lyrics by Stephen Sondheim
Treemonisha. Music and lyrics by Scott Joplin

Scenic Designer
☆ Boris Aronson, *Pacific Overtures*
Ben Edwards, *A Matter of Gravity*
David Mitchell, *Trelawny of the 'Wells'*
Tony Walton, *Chicago*

Costume Designer
Theoni V. Aldredge, *A Chorus Line*
☆ Florence Klotz, *Pacific Overtures*
Ann Roth, *The Royal Family*
Patricia Zipprodt, *Chicago*

Lighting Designer
Ian Calderon, *Trelawny of the 'Wells'*
Jules Fisher, *Chicago*
☆ Tharon Musser, *A Chorus Line*
Tharon Musser, *Pacific Overtures*

Choreographer
☆ Michael Bennet and Bob Avian, *A Chorus Line*
Patricia Birch, *Pacific Overtures*
Bob Fosse, *Chicago*
Billy Wilson, *Bubbling Brown Sugar*

Special Awards
☆ Mathilde Pincus, *Circle in the Square*
☆ Thomas H. Fitzgerald, *The Arena Stage*
☆ Richard Burton, *Equus*

1977

ACTOR (PLAY)
Tom Courtenay, *Otherwise Engaged*
Ben Gazzara, *Who's Afraid of Virginia Woolf?*
☆ Al Pacino, *The Basic Training of Pavlo Hummel*
Ralph Richardson, *No Man's Land*

ACTRESS (PLAY)
Colleen Dewhurst, *Who's Afraid of Virginia Woolf?*
☆ Julie Harris, *The Belle of Amherst*
Liv Ullmann, *Anna Christie*
Irene Worth, *The Cherry Orchard*

ACTOR (FEATURED ROLE—PLAY)
Bob Dishy, *Sly Fox*
Joe Fields, *The Basic Training of Pavlo Hummel*
Laurence Luckinbill, *The Shadow Box*
☆ Jonathan Pryce, *Comedians*

ACTRESS (FEATURED ROLE—PLAY)
☆ Trazana Beverley, *For Colored Girls Who Have Considered
    Suicide/When the Rainbow is Enuf*
Patricia Elliott, *The Shadow Box*
Rose Gregorio, *The Shadow Box*
Mary McCarty, *Anna Christie*

ACTOR (MUSICAL)
☆ Barry Bostwick, *The Robber Bridegroom*
Robert Guillaume, *Guys and Dolls*
Raul Julia, *Threepenny Opera*
Reid Shelton, *Annie*

ACTRESS (MUSICAL)
Clamma Dale, *Porgy and Bess*
Ernestine Jackson, *Guys and Dolls*
☆ Dorothy Loudon, *Annie*
Andrea McArdle, *Annie*

ACTOR (FEATURED ROLE—MUSICAL)
☆ Lenny Baker, *I Love My Wife*
David Kernan, *Side By Side By Sondheim*
Larry Marshall, *Porgy and Bess*
Ned Sherrin, *Side By Side By Sondheim*

ACTRESS (FEATURED ROLE—MUSICAL)
Ellen Green, *Threepenny Opera*

☆ Delores Hall, *Your Arm's Too Short To Box With God*
Millicent Martin, *Side By Side By Sondheim*
Julie N. McKenzie, *Side By Side By Sondheim*

PLAY

For Colored Girls Who Have Considered Suicide/When the Rainbow is Enuf by Ntozake Shange. Produced by Joseph Papp

Otherwise Engaged by Simon Gray. Produced by Michael Codron, Frank Milton, and James M. Nederlander

Streamers by David Rabe. Produced by Joseph Papp

☆ *The Shadow Box* by Michael Cristofer. Produced by Allan Francis, Ken Marsolais, Lester Osterman, and Leonard Soloway

DIRECTOR (PLAY)

☆ Gordon Davidson, *The Shadow Box*
Ulu Grosbard, *American Buffalo*
Mike Nichols, *Comedians*
Mike Nichols, *Streamers*

MUSICAL

☆ *Annie*. Produced by Lewis Allen, Mike Nichols, Irwin Meyer, and Stephen R. Friedman

Happy End. Produced by Michael Harvey and The Chelsea Theatre Center

I Love My Wife. Produced by Terry Allen Kramer and Harry Rigby in association with Joseph Kipness

Side By Side By Sondheim. Produced by Harold Prince in association with Ruth Mitchell

DIRECTOR (MUSICAL)

Vinnette Carroll, *Your Arm's Too Short To Box With God*
Martin Charnin, *Annie*
Jack O'Brien, *Porgy and Bess*
☆ Gene Saks, *I Love My Wife*

BOOK (MUSICAL)

☆ *Annie* by Thomas Meehan
Happy End by Elisabeth Hauptmann. Adaptation by Michael Feingold
I Love My Wife by Michael Stewart
Your Arm's Too Short To Box With God by Vinnette Carroll

SCORE

☆ *Annie*. Music by Charles Strouse, lyrics by Martin Charnin
Godspell. Music and lyrics by Stephen Schwartz
I Love My Wife. Music by Cy Coleman, lyrics by Michael Stewart

Happy End. Music by Kurt Weill, lyrics by Bertolt Brecht. Adapted by Michael Feingold

SCENIC DESIGNER
Santo Loquasto, *American Buffalo*
Santo Loquasto, *The Cherry Orchard*
☆ David Mitchell, *Annie*
Robert Randolph, *Porgy and Bess*

COSTUMER DESIGNER
☆ Theoni V. Aldredge, *Annie*
Theoni V. Aldredge, *Threepenny Opera*
☆ Santo Loquasto, *The Cherry Orchard*
Nancy Potts, *Porgy and Bess*

LIGHTING DESIGNER
John Bury, *No Man's Land*
Pat Collins, *Threepenny Opera*
Neil Peter Jampolis, *The Innocents*
☆ Jennifer Tipton, *The Cherry Orchard*

CHOREOGRAPHER
Talley Beatty, *Your Arm's Too Short To Box With God*
Patricia Birch, *Music Is*
☆ Peter Gennaro, *Annie*
Onna White, *I Love My Wife*

MOST INNOVATIVE PRODUCTION OF A REVIVAL
Guys and Dolls. Produced by Moe Septee in association with Victor H. Potamkin, Carmen F. Zollo, and Ashton Springer.
☆ *Porgy and Bess.* Produced by Sherwin M. Goldman and Houston Grand Opera
The Cherry Orchard. Produced by Joseph Papp
Threepenny Opera. Produced by Joseph Papp

SPECIAL AWARDS
☆ Lily Tomlin
☆ Barry Manilow
☆ Diana Ross
☆ National Theatre For The Deaf
☆ Mark Taper Forum
☆ Equity Library Theatre

1978

ACTOR (PLAY)
Hume Cronyn, *The Gin Game*
☆ Barnard Hughes, *Da*
Frank Langella, *Dracula*
Jason Robards, *A Touch of the Poet*

ACTRESS (PLAY)
Anne Bancroft, *Golda*
Anita Gillette, *Chapter Two*
Estelle Parsons, *Miss Margarida's Way*
☆ Jessica Tandy, *The Gin Game*

ACTOR (FEATURED ROLE—PLAY)
Morgan Freeman, *The Mighty Gents*
Victor Garber, *Deathtrap*
Cliff Gorman, *Chapter Two*
☆ Lester Rawlins, *Da*

ACTRESS (FEATURED ROLE—PLAY)
Starletta DuPois, *The Mighty Gents*
Swoosie Kurtz, *Tartuffe*
Marian Seldes, *Deathtrap*
☆ Ann Wedgeworth, *Chapter Two*

ACTOR (MUSICAL)
Eddie Bracken, *Hello, Dolly!*
☆ John Cullum, *On The Twentieth Century*
Barry Nelson, *The Act*
Gilbert Price, *Timbuktu!*

ACTRESS (MUSICAL)
Madeline Kahn, *On The Twentieth Century*
Eartha Kitt, *Timbuktu!*
☆ Liza Minnelli, *The Act*
Frances Sternhagen, *Angel*

ACTOR (FEATURED ROLE—MUSICAL)
Steven Boockvor, *Working*
Wayne Cilento, *Dancin'*
Rex Everhart, *Working*
☆ Kevin Kline, *On The Twentieth Century*

ACTRESS (FEATURED ROLE—MUSICAL)
☆ Nell Carter, *Ain't Misbehavin'*
Imogene Coca, *On The Twentieth Century*

Ann Reinking, *Dancin'*
Charlaine Woodard, *Ain't Misbehavin'*

PLAY

Chapter Two by Neil Simon. Produced by Emanuel Azenberg
☆ *Da* by Hugh Leonard. Produced by Lester Osterman, Marilyn Strauss, and Marc Howard
Deathtrap by Ira Levin. Produced by Alfred De Liagre, Jr., and Roger L. Stevens
The Gin Game by D. L. Coburn. Produced by The Shubert Organization, Hume Cronyn, and Mike Nichols

DIRECTOR (PLAY)

☆ Melvin Bernhardt, *Da*
Robert Moore, *Deathtrap*
Mike Nichols, *The Gin Game*
Dennis Rosa, *Dracula*

MUSICAL

☆ *Ain't Misbehavin'*. Produced by Emanuel Azenberg, Dasha Epstein, The Shubert Organization, Jane Gaynor, and Ron Dante
Dancin'. Produced by Jules Fisher, The Shubert Organization, and Columbia Pictures
On The Twentieth Century. Produced by The Producers Circle 2, Inc. (Robert Fryer, Mary Lea Johnson, James Cresson, and Martin Richards), Joseph Harris, and Ira Bernstein
Runaways. Produced by Joseph Papp

DIRECTOR (MUSICAL)

Bob Fosse, *Dancin'*
☆ Richard Maltby, Jr., *Ain't Misbehavin'*
Harold Prince, *On The Twentieth Century*
Elizabeth Swados, *Runaways*

BOOK (MUSICAL)

A History of the American Film by Christopher Durang
☆ *On The Twentieth Century* by Betty Comden and Adolph Green
Runaways by Elizabeth Swados
Working by Stephen Schwartz

SCORE

The Act. Music by John Kander, lyrics by Fred Ebb
☆ *On The Twentieth Century*. Music by Cy Coleman, lyrics by Betty Comden and Adolph Green
Runaways. Music and lyrics by Elizabeth Swados
Working. Music and lyrics by Craig Carnelia, Micki Grant, Mary Rodgers/Susan Birkenhead, Stephen Schwartz, and James Taylor

SCENIC DESIGNER
Zack Brown, *The Importance of Being Ernest*
Edward Gorey, *Dracula*
David Mitchell, *Working*
☆ Robin Wagner, *On The Twentieth Century*

COSTUME DESIGNER
☆ Edward Gorey, *Dracula*
Halston, *The Act*
Geoffrey Holder, *Timbuktu!*
Willa Kim, *Dancin'*

LIGHTING DESIGNER
Jules Fisher, *Beatlemania*
☆ Jules Fisher, *Dancin'*
Tharon Musser, *The Act*
Ken Billington, *Working*

CHOREOGRAPHER
Arthur Faria, *Ain't Misbehavin'*
☆ Bob Fosse, *Dancin'*
Ron Lewis, *The Act*
Elizabeth Swados, *Runaways*

MOST INNOVATIVE PRODUCTION OF A REVIVAL
☆ *Dracula.* Produced by Jujamcyn Theatre, Elizabeth I. McCann,
    John Wulp, Victor Lurie, Nelle Nugent, and Max Weitzenhoffer
Tartuffe. Produced by Circle in the Square
Timbuktu! Produced by Luther Davis
A Touch of the Poet. Produced by Elliot Martin

SPECIAL AWARD
☆ The Long Wharf Theatre

1979

ACTOR (PLAY)
Philip Anglim, *The Elephant Man*
☆ Tom Conti, *Whose Life Is It Anyway?*
Jack Lemmon, *Tribute*
Alec McCowen, *St. Mark's Gospel*

ACTRESS (PLAY)
Jane Alexander, *First Monday In October*
☆ Constance Cummings, *Wings*

☆ Carole Shelley, *The Elephant Man*
Frances Sternhagen, *On Golden Pond*

ACTOR (FEATURED ROLE—PLAY)
Bob Balaban, *The Inspector General*
☆ Michael Gough, *Bedroom Farce*
Joseph Maher, *Spokesong*
Edward James Olmos, *Zoot Suit*

ACTRESS (FEATURED ROLE—PLAY)
☆ Joan Hickson, *Bedroom Farce*
Laurie Kennedy, *Man And Superman*
Susan Littler, *Bedroom Farce*
Mary-Joan Negro, *Wings*

ACTOR (MUSICAL)
☆ Len Cariou, *Sweeney Todd*
Vincent Gardenia, *Ballroom*
Joel Grey, *The Grand Tour*
Robert Klein, *They're Playing Our Song*

ACTRESS (MUSICAL)
Tovah Feldshuh, *Sarava*
☆ Angela Lansbury, *Sweeney Todd*
Dorothy Loudon, *Ballroom*
Alexis Smith, *Platinum*

ACTOR (FEATURED ROLE—MUSICAL)
Richard Cox, *Platinum*
☆ Henderson Forsythe, *The Best Little Whorehouse in Texas*
Gregory Hines, *Eubie!*
Ron Holgate, *The Grand Tour*

ACTRESS (FEATURED ROLE—MUSICAL)
Joan Ellis, *The Best Little Whorehouse in Texas*
☆ Carlin Glynn, *The Best Little Whorehouse in Texas*
Millicent Martin, *King Of Hearts*
Maxine Sullivan, *My Old Friends*

PLAY
Bedroom Farce by Alan Ayckbourn. Produced by Robert
    Whitehead, Roger L. Stevens, George W. George, and Frank
    Milton
☆ *The Elephant Man* by Bernard Pomerance. Produced by
    Richmond Crinkley, Elizabeth I. McCann, and Nelle Nugent
Whose Life Is It Anyway? by Brian Clark. Produced by Emanuel
    Azenberg, James Nederlander, and Ray Cooney
Wings by Arthur Kopit. Produced by The Kennedy Center

DIRECTOR (PLAY)
Alan Ayckbourn and Peter Hall, *Bedroom Farce*
Paul Giovanni, *The Crucifer of Blood*
☆ Jack Hofsiss, *The Elephant Man*
Michael Lindsay-Hogg, *Whose Life Is It Anyway?*

MUSICAL
Ballroom. Produced by Michael Bennett, Bob Avian, Bernard
    Gersten, and Susan MacNair
☆ *Sweeney Todd.* Produced by Richard Barr, Charles Woodward,
    Robert Fryer, Mary Lea Johnson, and Martin Richards
The Best Little Whorehouse in Texas. Produced by Universal Pictures
They're Playing Our Song. Produced by Emanuel Azenberg

DIRECTOR (MUSICAL)
Michael Bennett, *Ballroom*
Peter Masterson and Tommy Tune, *The Best Little Whorehouse in*
    Texas
Robert Moore, *They're Playing Our Song*
☆ Harold Prince, *Sweeney Todd*

BOOK (MUSICAL)
Ballroom by Jerome Kass
☆ *Sweeney Todd* by Hugh Wheeler
The Best Little Whorehouse in Texas by Larry L. King and Peter
    Masterson
They're Playing Our Song by Neil Simon

SCORE
Carmelina. Music by Burton Lane, lyrics by Alan Jay Lerner
Eubie! Music by Eubie Blak, lyrics by Noble Sissle, Andy Razaf, F.
    E. Miller, Johnny Brandon, and Jim Europe
☆ *Sweeney Todd.* Music and lyrics by Stephen Sondheim
The Grand Tour. Music and lyrics by Jerry Herman

SCENIC DESIGNER
Karl Eigsti, *Knockout*
David Jenkins, *The Elephant Man*
☆ Eugene Lee, *Sweeney Todd*
John Wulp, *The Crucifer of Blood*

COSTUME DESIGNER
Theoni V. Aldredge, *Ballroom*
☆ Franne Lee, *Sweeney Todd*
Ann Roth, *The Crucifer of Blood*
Julie Weiss, *The Elephant Man*

LIGHTING DESIGNER
Ken Billington, *Sweeney Todd*
Beverly Emmons, *The Elephant Man*
☆ Roger Morgan, *The Crucifer of Blood*
Tharon Musser, *Ballroom*

CHOREOGRAPHER
☆ Michael Bennett and Bob Avian, *Ballroom*
Henry LeTang and Billy Wilson, *Eubie!*
Dan Siretta, *Whoopee!*
Tommy Tune, *The Best Little Whorehouse in Texas*

SPECIAL AWARDS
☆ Henry Fonda
☆ Walter F. Diehl
☆ Eugene O'Neill Memorial Theatre Center
☆ American Conservatory Theater

The 1980s

"**I**t was Mother's Day in Paris. I was thinking, 'what shall I get her?' And, it came . . . the most wonderful present, 'My Tony® Award.' It was, for her, the proudest moment of her daughter's life, and for me, the happiest. I shall never forget this memorable moment, and I want to thank you for making it possible."

Liliane Montevecchi

"Sharing a limo to the theatre with the playwright Mark Medoff (who also won)—quiet tension, defense mechanisms at the ready. When they called my name, mostly it was about trying to remain standing despite the violent shaking of my legs. Back in the limo—what a contrast! Screaming, laughing, crying—are these the same people? And now—still—what an incredible honor."

Phyllis Frelich

1980

ACTOR (PLAY)
Charles Brown, *Home*
Gerald Hiken, *Strider*
Judd Hirsch, *Talley's Folly*
☆ John Rubinstein, *Children of a Lesser God*

ACTRESS (PLAY)
Blythe Danner, *Betrayal*
☆ Phyllis Frelich, *Children of a Lesser God*
Maggie Smith, *Night and Day*
Anne Twomey, *Nuts*

ACTOR (FEATURED ROLE—PLAY)
David Dukes, *Bent*
George Hearn, *Watch on the Rhine*
Earle Hyman, *The Lady from Dubuque*
Joseph Maher, *Night and Day*
☆ David Rounds, *Morning's at Seven*

ACTRESS (FEATURED ROLE—PLAY)
Maureen Anderman, *The Lady from Dubuque*
Pamela Burrell, *Strider*
Lois de Banzie, *Morning's at Seven*
☆ Dinah Manoff, *I Ought To Be In Pictures*

ACTOR (MUSICAL)
☆ Jim Dale, *Barnum*
Gregory Hines, *Comin' Uptown*
Mickey Rooney, *Sugar Babies*
Giorgio Tozzi, *The Most Happy Fella*

ACTRESS (MUSICAL)
Christine Andreas, *Oklahoma!*
Sandy Duncan, *Peter Pan*
☆ Patti LuPone, *Evita*
Ann Miller, *Sugar Babies*

ACTOR (FEATURED ROLE—MUSICAL)
David Garrison, *A Day in Hollywood/A Night in the Ukraine*
Harry Groener, *Oklahoma!*
Bob Gunton, *Evita*
☆ Mandy Patinkin, *Evita*

ACTRESS (FEATURED ROLE—MUSICAL)
Debbie Allen, *West Side Story*

Glenn Close, *Barnum*
Jossie de Guzman, *West Side Story*
☆ Priscilla Lopez, *A Day in Hollywood/A Night in the Ukraine*

PLAY
Bent by Martin Sherman. Produced by Jack Schlissel and Steven
    Steinlauf
☆ *Children of a Lesser God* by Mark Medoff. Produced by Emanuel
    Azenberg, The Shubert Organization, Dasha Epstein, and
    Ron Dante
Home by Samm-Art Williams. Produced by Elizabeth I. McCann,
    Nelle Nugent, Gerald S. Krone, and Ray Larsen
Talley's Folly by Lanford Wilson. Produced by Nancy Cooperstein,
    Porter Van Zandt, and Marc Howard

DIRECTOR (PLAY)
Gordon Davidson, *Children of a Lesser God*
Peter Hall, *Betrayal*
Marshall W. Mason, *Talley's Folly*
☆ Vivian Matalon, *Morning's at Seven*

MUSICAL
A Day in Hollywood/A Night in the Ukraine. Produced by Alexander H.
    Cohen and Hildy Parks
Barnum. Produced by Judy Gordon, Cy Coleman, Lois Rosenfield,
    and Maurice Rosenfield
☆ *Evita.* Produced by Robert Stigwood
Sugar Babies. Produced by Terry Allen Kramer and Harry Rigby

DIRECTOR (MUSICAL)
Ernest Flatt and Rudy Tronto, *Sugar Babies*
Joe Layton, *Barnum*
☆ Harold Prince, *Evita*
Tommy Tune, *A Day in Hollywood/A Night in the Ukraine*

BOOK (MUSICAL)
A Day in Hollywood/A Night in the Ukraine by Dick Vosburgh
Barnum by Mark Bramble
☆ *Evita* by Tim Rice
Sugar Babies by Ralph G. Allen and Harry Rigby

SCORE
A Day in Hollywood/A Night in the Ukraine. Music by Frank Lazarus,
    lyrics by Dick Vosburgh
Barnum. Music by Cy Coleman, lyrics by Michael Stewart
☆ *Evita.* Music by Andrew Lloyd Webber, lyrics by Tim Rice
Sugar Babies. Music and lyrics by Arthur Malvin

SCENIC DESIGNER
☆ John Lee Beatty, *Talley's Folly*
☆ David Mitchell, *Barnum*
Timothy O'Brien and Tazeena Firth, *Evita*
Tony Walton, *A Day in Hollywood/A Night in the Ukraine*

COSTUME DESIGNER
☆ Theoni V. Aldredge, *Barnum*
Pierre Balmain, *Happy New Year*
Timothy O'Brien and Tazeena Firth, *Evita*
Raoul Pène du Bois, *Sugar Babies*

LIGHTING DESIGNER
Beverly Emmons, *A Day in Hollywood/A Night in the Ukraine*
☆ David Hersey, *Evita*
Craig Miller, *Barnum*
Dennis Parichy, *Talley's Folly*

CHOREOGRAPHER
Ernest Flatt, *Sugar Babies*
Larry Fuller, *Evita*
Joe Layton, *Barnum*
☆ Tommy Tune and Thommie Walsh, *A Day in Hollywood/A Night in the Ukraine*

REPRODUCTION (PLAY OR MUSICAL)
Major Barbara
☆ *Morning's At Seven*
Peter Pan
West Side Story

SPECIAL AWARDS
☆ Mary Tyler Moore
☆ Actors Theatre of Louisville
☆ Goodspeed Opera House

1981

ACTOR (PLAY)
Tim Curry, *Amadeus*
Roy Dotrice, *A Life*
☆ Ian McKellen, *Amadeus*
Jack Weston, *The Floating Light Bulb*

ACTRESS (PLAY)
Glenda Jackson, *Rose*
☆ Jane Lapotaire, *Piaf*
Eva Le Gallienne, *To Grandmother's House We Go*
Elizabeth Taylor, *The Little Foxes*

ACTOR (FEATURED ROLE—PLAY)
Tom Aldredge, *The Little Foxes*
☆ Brian Backer, *The Floating Light Bulb*
Adam Redfield, *A Life*
Shepperd Strudwick, *To Grandmother's House We Go*

ACTRESS (FEATURED ROLE—PLAY)
☆ Swoosie Kurtz, *Fifth of July*
Maureen Stapleton, *The Little Foxes*
Jessica Tandy, *Rose*
Zoe Wanamaker, *Piaf*

ACTOR (MUSICAL)
Gregory Hines, *Sophisticated Ladies*
☆ Kevin Kline, *The Pirates of Penzance*
George Rose, *The Pirates of Penzance*
Martin Vidnovic, *Brigadoon*

ACTRESS (MUSICAL)
☆ Lauren Bacall, *Woman of the Year*
Meg Bussert, *Brigadoon*
Chita Rivera, *Bring Back Birdie*
Linda Ronstadt, *The Pirates of Penzance*

ACTOR (FEATURED ROLE—MUSICAL)
Tony Azito, *The Pirates of Penzance*
☆ Hinton Battle, *Sophisticated Ladies*
Lee Roy Reams, *42nd Street*
Paxton Whitehead, *Camelot*

ACTRESS (FEATURED ROLE—MUSICAL)
☆ Marilyn Cooper, *Woman of the Year*
Phyllis Hyman, *Sophisticated Ladies*
Wanda Richert, *42nd Street*
Lynne Thigpen, *Tintypes*

PLAY
A Lesson From Aloes by Athol Fugard. Produced by Jay J. Cohen, Richard Press, Louis Bush Hager Associates, and Yale Repertory Theater

A Life by Hugh Leonard. Produced by Lester Osterman, Richard Horner, Hinks Shimberg, and Freydberg-Cutler-Diamond Productions

☆ *Amadeus* by Peter Shaffer. Produced by The Shubert Organization, Elizabeth I. McCann, Nelle Nugent, and Roger S. Berlind

Fifth of July by Lanford Wilson. Produced by Jerry Arrow, Robert Lussier, and Warner Theater Productions

DIRECTOR (PLAY)
Peter Coe, *A Life*
☆ Peter Hall, *Amadeus*
Marshall W. Mason, *Fifth of July*
Austin Pendleton, *The Little Foxes*

MUSICAL
☆ *42nd Street*. Produced by David Merrick
Sophisticated Ladies. Produced by Roger S. Berlind, Manheim Fox, Sondra Gilman, Burton L. Litwin, Louise Westergaard, Belwin Mills Publishing Corporation, and Norzar Productions, Inc.
Tintypes. Produced by Richmond Crinkley, Royal Pardon Productions, Ivan Bloch, Larry J. Silva, Eve Skina, and Joan F. Tobin
Woman of the Year. Produced by Lawrence Kasha, David S. Landay, James M. Nederlander, Warner Theater Productions, Claire Nichtern, Carole J. Shorenstein, and Stewart F. Lane

DIRECTOR (MUSICAL)
Gower Champion, *42nd Street*
☆ Wilford Leach, *The Pirates of Penzance*
Robert Moore, *Woman of the Year*
Michael Smuin, *Sophisticated Ladies*

BOOK (MUSICAL)
42nd Street by Michael Stewart and Mark Bramble
The Moony Shapiro Songbook by Monty Norman and Julian More
Tintypes by Mary Kyte
☆ *Woman of the Year* by Peter Stone

SCORE
Charlie and Algernon. Music by Charles Strouse, lyrics by David Rogers
Copperfield. Music and lyrics by Al Kasha and Joel Hirschhorn
Shakespeare's Cabaret. Music by Lance Mulcahy
☆ *Woman of the Year*. Music by John Kander, lyrics by Fred Ebb

SCENIC DESIGNERS
John Lee Beatty, *Fifth of July*
☆ John Bury, *Amadeus*
Santo Loquasto, *The Suicide*
David Mitchell, *Can-Can*

COSTUME DESIGNER
Theoni V. Aldredge, *42nd Street*
John Bury, *Amadeus*
☆ Willa Kim, *Sophisticated Ladies*
Franca Squarciapino, *Can-Can*

LIGHTING DESIGNER
☆ John Bury, *Amadeus*
Tharon Musser, *42nd Street*
Dennis Parichy, *Fifth of July*
Jennifer Tipton, *Sophisticated Ladies*

CHOREOGRAPHER
☆ Gower Champion, *42nd Street*
Graciela Daniele, *The Pirates of Penzance*
Henry le Tang, Donald McKayle, and Michael Smuin, *Sophisticated Ladies*
Roland Petit, *Can-Can*

REPRODUCTION (PLAY OR MUSICAL)
Brigadoon
Camelot
The Little Foxes
☆ *The Pirates of Penzance*

SPECIAL AWARDS
☆ Lena Horne
☆ Trinity Square Repertory Company

1982

ACTOR (PLAY)
Tom Courtenay, *The Dresser*
Milo O'Shea, *Mass Appeal*
Christopher Plummer, *Othello*
☆ Roger Rees, *The Life and Adventures of Nicholas Nickleby*

ACTRESS (PLAY)
☆ Zoe Caldwell, *Medea*
Katharine Hepburn, *The West Side Waltz*

Geraldine Page, A*gnes of God*
Amanda Plummer, A T*aste of Honey*

ACTOR (FEATURED ROLE—PLAY)
Richard Kavanaugh, T*he Hothouse*
☆ Zakes Mokae, '*Master Harold*' . . . *and the Boys*
Edward Petherbridge, T*he Life and Adventures of Nicholas Nickleby*
David Threlfall, T*he Life and Adventures of Nicholas Nickleby*

ACTRESS (FEATURED ROLE—PLAY)
Judith Anderson, *Medea*
Mia Dillon, *Crimes of the Heart*
Mary Beth Hurt, *Crimes of the Heart*
☆ Amanda Plummer, A*gnes of God*

ACTOR (MUSICAL)
Herschel Bernardi, *Fiddler on the Roof*
Victor Garber, *Little Me*
☆ Ben Harney, *Dreamgirls*
Raul Julia, *Nine*

ACTRESS (MUSICAL)
☆ Jennifer Holliday, *Dreamgirls*
Lisa Mordente, *Marlowe*
Mary Gordon Murray, *Little Me*
Sheryl Lee Ralph, *Dreamgirls*

ACTOR (FEATURED ROLE—MUSICAL)
Obba Babatunde, *Dreamgirls*
☆ Cleavant Derricks, *Dreamgirls*
David Alan Grier, T*he First*
Bill Hutton, *Joseph and The Amazing Technicolor Dreamcoat*

ACTRESS (FEATURED ROLE—MUSICAL)
Karen Akers, *Nine*
Laurie Beechman, *Joseph and The Amazing Technicolor Dreamcoat*
☆ Liliane Montevecchi, *Nine*
Anita Morris, *Nine*

PLAY
Crimes of the Heart, by Beth Henley. Produced by Warner Theater
 Productions, Inc., Claire Nichtern, Mary Lea Johnson, Martin
 Richards, and Francine LeFrak
T*he Dresser*, by Ronald Harwood. Produced by James M.
 Nederlander, Elizabeth I. McCann, Nelle Nugent, Warner
 Theater Productions, Inc., and Michael Codron

'*Master Harold*' . . . *and the Boys* by Athol Fugard. Produced by The
    Shubert Organization, Freydberg/Bloch Productions, Dasha
    Epstein, Emanuel Azenberg and David Geffen
☆ *The Life and Adventures of Nicholas Nickleby* by David Edgar.
    Produced by James M. Nederlander, The Shubert
    Organization, Elizabeth I. McCann, and Nelle Nugent

DIRECTOR (PLAY)
Melvin Bernhardt, *Crimes of the Heart*
Geraldine Fitzgerald, *Mass Appeal*
Athol Fugard, '*Master Harold*' . . . *and the Boys*
☆ Trevor Nunn/John Caird, *The Life and Adventures of Nicholas
    Nickleby*

MUSICAL
Dreamgirls. Produced by Michael Bennett, Bob Avian, Geffen
    Records, and The Shubert Organization
Joseph and The Amazing Technicolor Dreamcoat. Produced by Zev
    Bufman, Susan R. Rose, Melvin J. Estrin, Sidney Shlenker,
    and Gail Berman
☆ *Nine*. Produced by Michel Stuart, Harvey J. Klaris, Roger S.
    Berlind, James M. Nederlander, Francine LeFrak, and
    Kenneth D. Greenblatt
Pump Boys and Dinettes. Dodger Productions, Louis Busch Hager,
    Marilyn Strauss, Kate Studley, Warner Theater Productions,
    Inc., and Max Weitzenhoffer

DIRECTOR (MUSICAL)
Michael Bennett, *Dreamgirls*
Martin Charnin, *The First*
Tony Tanner, *Joseph and The Amazing Technicolor Dreamcoat*
☆ Tommy Tune, *Nine*

BOOK (MUSICAL)
☆ *Dreamgirls* by Tom Eyen
Joseph and The Amazing Technicolor Dreamcoat by Tim Rice
Nine by Arthur Kopit
The First by Joel Siegel and Martin Charnin

SCORE
Dreamgirls. Music by Henry Krieger, lyrics by Tom Eyen
Joseph and The Amazing Technicolor Dreamcoat. Music by Andrew
    Lloyd Webber, lyrics by Tim Rice
Merrily We Roll Along. Music and lyrics by Stephen Sondheim
☆ *Nine*. Music and lyrics by Maury Yeston

SCENIC DESIGNERS
Ben Edwards, *Medea*
Lawrence Miller, *Nine*
☆ John Napier/Dermot Hayes, *The Life and Adventures of Nicholas Nickleby*
Robin Wagner, *Dreamgirls*

COSTUME DESIGNER
Theoni V. Aldredge, *Dreamgirls*
Jane Greenwood, *Medea*
☆ William Ivey Long, *Nine*
John Napier, *The Life and Adventures of Nicholas Nickleby*

LIGHTING DESIGNER
Martin Aronstein, *Medea*
David Hersey, *The Life and Adventures of Nicholas Nickleby*
Marcia Madeira, *Nine*
☆ Tharon Musser, *Dreamgirls*

CHOREOGRAPHER
☆ Michael Bennett/Michael Peters, *Dreamgirls*
Peter Gennaro, *Little Me*
Tony Tanner, *Joseph and The Amazing Technicolor Dreamcoat*
Tommy Tune, *Nine*

REPRODUCTION (PLAY OR MUSICAL)
A *Taste of Honey*
Medea
My Fair Lady
☆ *Othello*

SPECIAL AWARDS
☆ The Guthrie Theatre
☆ The Actors' Fund of America

1983

ACTOR (PLAY)
Jeffrey DeMunn, *K2*
☆ Harvey Fierstein, *Torch Song Trilogy*
Edward Herrmann, *Plenty*
Tony Lo Bianco, *A View From The Bridge*

ACTRESS (PLAY)
Kathy Bates, *'Night, Mother*
Kate Nelligan, *Plenty*

Anne Pitoniak, *'Night, Mother*
☆ Jessica Tandy, *Foxfire*

ACTOR (FEATURED ROLE—PLAY)
☆ Matthew Broderick, *Brighton Beach Memoirs*
Zeljko Ivanek, *Brighton Beach Memoirs*
George N. Martin, *Plenty*
Stephen Moore, *All's Well That Ends Well*

ACTRESS (FEATURED ROLE—PLAY)
Elizabeth Franz, *Brighton Beach Memoirs*
Roxanne Hart, *Passion*
☆ Judith Ivey, *Steaming*
Margaret Tyzack, *All's Well That Ends Well*

ACTOR (MUSICAL)
Al Green, *Your Arm's Too Short To Box With God*
George Hearn, *A Doll's Life*
Michael V. Smartt, *Porgy & Bess*
☆ Tommy Tune, *My One and Only*

ACTRESS (MUSICAL)
☆ Natalia Makarova, *On Your Toes*
Lonette McKee, *Show Boat*
Chita Rivera, *Merlin*
Twiggy, *My One and Only*

ACTOR (FEATURED ROLE—MUSICAL)
☆ Charles "Honi" Coles, *My One and Only*
Harry Groener, *Cats*
Stephen Hanan, *Cats*
Lara Teeter, *On Your Toes*

ACTRESS (FEATURED ROLE—MUSICAL)
Christine Andreas, *On Your Toes*
☆ Betty Buckley, *Cats*
Karla Burns, *Show Boat*
Denny Dillon, *My One and Only*

PLAY
Angels Fall by Lanford Wilson. Produced by Elliot Martin, Circle Repertory Co., Lucille Lortel, The Shubert Organization, and The Kennedy Center
'Night, Mother by Marsha Norman. Produced by Dann Byck, Wendell Cherry, The Shubert Organization and Frederick M. Zollo
Plenty by David Hare. Produced by Joseph Papp

☆ *Torch Song Trilogy* Harvey Fierstein. Produced by Kenneth Waissman, Martin Markinson, Lawrence Lane, John Glines, BetMar, and Donald Tick

DIRECTOR (PLAY)
Marhsall W. Mason, *Angels Fall*
Tom Moore, *'Night, Mother*
Trevor Nunn, *All's Well That Ends Well*
☆ Gene Saks, *Brighton Beach Memoirs*

MUSICAL
Blues in the Night. Produced by Mitchell Maxwell, Alan J. Schuster, Fred H. Krones, and M² Entertainment, Inc.
☆ *Cats*. Produced by Cameron Mackintosh, The Really Useful Company, Inc., David Geffen, and The Shubert Organization
Merlin. Produced by Ivan Reitman, Columbia Pictures Stage Productions, Inc., Marvin A. Krauss, and James M. Nederlander
My One and Only. Paramount Theatre Productions, Francine LeFrak, and Kenneth-Mark Productions

DIRECTOR (MUSICAL)
Michael Kahn, *Show Boat*
☆ Trevor Nunn, *Cats*
Ivan Reitman, *Merlin*
Tommy Tune, Thommie Walsh, *My One and Only*

BOOK (MUSICAL)
A *Doll's Life* by Betty Comden and Adolph Green
☆ *Cats* by T. S. Eliot
Merlin by Richard Levinson and William Link
My One and Only by Peter Stone and Timothy S. Mayer

SCORE
A *Doll's Life*. Music by Larry Grossman, lyrics by Betty Comden and Adolph Green
☆ *Cats*. Music by Andrew Lloyd Webber, lyrics by T. S. Eliot
Merlin. Music by Elmer Bernstein, lyrics by Don Black
Seven Brides for Seven Brothers. Music by Gene de Paul, Al Kasha, and Joel Hirschhorn, lyrics by Johnny Mercer, Al Kasha and Joel Hirschhorn

SCENIC DESIGNER
John Gunter, *All's Well That Ends Well*
☆ Ming Cho Lee, *K2*
David Mitchell, *Foxfire*
John Napier, *Cats*

COSTUME DESIGNER
Lindy Hemming, *All's Well That Ends Well*
☆ John Napier, *Cats*
Rita Ryack, *My One and Only*
Patricia Zipprodt, *Alice in Wonderland*

LIGHTING DESIGNER
Ken Billington, *Foxfire*
Robert Bryan, *All's Well That Ends Well*
☆ David Hersey, *Cats*
Allen Lee Hughes, *K2*

CHOREOGRAPHER
George Faison, *Porgy & Bess*
Gillian Lynne, *Cats*
Donald Saddler, *On Your Toes*
☆ Tommy Tune, Thommie Walsh, *My One and Only*

REPRODUCTION
All's Well That Ends Well
A View From The Bridge
The Caine Mutiny Court-Martial
☆ *On Your Toes*

SPECIAL AWARDS
☆ The Theatre Collection, Museum of the City of New York
☆ Shakespearean Festival Association

1984

ACTOR (PLAY)
☆ Jeremy Irons, *The Real Thing*
Calvin Levels, *Open Admissions*
Rex Harrison, *Heartbreak House*
Ian McKellen, *Ian McKellen Acting Shakespeare*

ACTRESS (PLAY)
☆ Glenn Close, *The Real Thing*
Rosemary Harris, *Heartbreak House*
Linda Hunt, *End of the World*
Kate Nelligan, *A Moon for the Misbegotten*

ACTOR (FEATURED ROLE—PLAY)
Philip Bosco, *Heartbreak House*
☆ Joe Mantegna, *Glengarry Glen Ross*

Robert Prosky, *Glengarry Glen Ross*
Douglas Seale, *Noises Off*

Actress (Featured Role—Play)
☆ Christine Baranski, *The Real Thing*
Jo Henderson, *Play Memory*
Dana Ivey, *Heartbreak House*
Deborah Rush, *Noises Off*

Actor (Musical)
Gene Barry, *La Cage aux Folles*
☆ George Hearn, *La Cage aux Folles*
Ron Moody, *Oliver!*
Mandy Patinkin, *Sunday in the Park with George*

Actress (Musical)
Rhetta Hughes, *Amen Corner*
Liza Minnelli, *The Rink*
Bernadette Peters, *Sunday in the Park with George*
☆ Chita Rivera, *The Rink*

Actor (Featured Role—Musical)
☆ Hinton Battle, *The Tap Dance Kid*
Stephen Geoffreys, *The Human Comedy*
Todd Graff, *Baby*
Samuel E. Wright, *The Tap Dance Kid*

Actress (Featured Role—Musical)
Martine Allard, *The Tap Dance Kid*
Liz Callaway, *Baby*
Dana Ivey, *Sunday in the Park with George*
☆ Lila Kedrova, *Zorba*

Play
Glengarry Glen Ross by David Mamet. Produced by Elliot Martin, The Shubert Organization, Arnold Bernhard, and The Goodman Theater
Noises Off by Michael Frayn. Produced by James Nederlander, Robert Fryer, Jerome Minskoff, The Kennedy Center, Michael Codron, Jonathan Farkas, and MTM Enterprises, Inc.
Play Memory by Joanna Glass. Produced by Alexander H. Cohen and Hildy Parks
☆ *The Real Thing* by Tom Stoppard. Produced by Emanuel Azenberg, The Shubert Organization, Icarus Productions, Byron Goldman, Ivan Bloch, Roger Berlind, and Michael Codron

DIRECTOR (PLAY)

Michael Blakemore, *Noises Off*
David Leveaux, *A Moon for the Misbegotten*
Gregory Mosher, *Glengarry Glen Ross*
☆ Mike Nichols, *The Real Thing*

MUSICAL

Baby. Produced by James B. Freydberg, Ivan Bloch, Kenneth-John Productions, Suzanne J. Schwartz, and Manuscript Productions
☆ *La Cage aux Folles*. Produced by Allan Carr, Kenneth D. Greenblatt, Marvin A. Krauss, Steward F. Lane, James M. Nederlander, Martin Richards, Barry Brown, and Fritz Holt
Sunday in the Park with George. Produced by The Shubert Organization and Emanuel Azenberg
The Tap Dance Kid. Produced by Stanley White, Evelyn Barron, Harvey J. Klaris, and Michel Stuart

DIRECTOR (MUSICAL)

James Lapine, *Sunday in the Park with George*
☆ Arthur Laurents, *La Cage aux Folles*
Richard Maltby, Jr., *Baby*
Vivian Matalon, *The Tap Dance Kid*

BOOK (MUSICAL)

Baby by Sybille Pearson
☆ *La Cage aux Folles* by Harvey Fierstein
Sunday in the Park with George by James Lapine
The Tap Dance Kid by Charles Blackwell

SCORE (MUSICAL)

Baby. Music by David Shire, lyrics by Richard Maltby, Jr.
☆ *La Cage aux Folles*. Music and lyrics by Jerry Herman
The Rink. Music by John Kander, lyrics by Fred Ebb
Sunday in the Park with George. Music and lyrics by Stephen Sondheim

SCENIC DESIGNER

Clarke Dunham, *End of the World*
Peter Larkin, *The Rink*
☆ Tony Straiges, *Sunday in the Park with George*
Tony Walton, *The Real Thing*

COSTUME DESIGNER

☆ Theoni V. Aldredge, *La Cage aux Folles*
Jane Greenwood, *Heartbreak House*

Anthea Sylbert, *The Real Thing*
Patricia Zipprodt and Ann Hould-Ward, *Sunday in the Park with George*

LIGHTING DESIGNER
Ken Billington, *End of the World*
Jules Fisher, *La Cage aux Folles*
☆ Richard Nelson, *Sunday in the Park with George*
Marc B. Weiss, *A Moon for the Misbegotten*

CHOREOGRAPHER
Wayne Cilento, *Baby*
Graciela Daniels, *The Rink*
☆ Danny Daniels, *The Tap Dance Kid*
Scott Salmon, *La Cage aux Folles*

REPRODUCTION
American Buffalo
☆ *Death of a Salesman*
Heartbreak House
A Moon for the Misbegotten

SPECIAL AWARDS
☆ San Diego Old Globe Theatre
☆ *La Tragedie de Carmen*
☆ Al Hirschfeld (Brooks Atkinson Award)
☆ Peter Feller

1985

ACTOR (PLAY)
Jim Dale, *Joe Egg*
Jonathan Hogan, *As Is*
☆ Derek Jacobi, *Much Ado About Nothing*
John Lithgow, *Requiem for a Heavyweight*

ACTRESS (PLAY)
☆ Stockard Channing, *Joe Egg*
Sinead Cusack, *Much Ado About Nothing*
Rosemary Harris, *Pack of Lies*
Glenda Jackson, *Strange Interlude*

ACTOR (FEATURED ROLE—PLAY)
Charles S. Dutton, *Ma Rainey's Black Bottom*
William Hurt, *Hurlyburly*

☆ Barry Miller, *Biloxi Blues*
Edward Petherbridge, *Strange Interlude*

ACTRESS (FEATURED ROLE—PLAY)
Joanna Gleason, *Joe Egg*
☆ Judith Ivey, *Hurlyburly*
Theresa Merritt, *Ma Rainey's Black Bottom*
Sigourney Weaver, *Hurlyburly*

ACTOR (MUSICAL)
Category eliminated

ACTRESS (MUSICAL)
Category eliminated

ACTOR (FEATURED ROLE—MUSICAL)
René Auberjonois, *Big River*
Daniel H. Jenkins, *Big River*
Kurt Knudson, *Take Me Along*
☆ Ron Richardson, *Big River*

ACTRESS (FEATURED ROLE—MUSICAL)
Evalyn Baron, *Quilters*
☆ Leilani Jones, *Grind*
Mary Beth Peil, *The King and I*
Lenka Peterson, *Quilters*

PLAY
As Is by William M. Hoffman. Produced by John Glines/Lawrence
    Lane, Lucille Lortel, and The Shubert Organization
☆ *Biloxi Blues* by Neil Simon. Produced by Emanuel Azenberg,
    and the Center Theater Group/Ahmanson Theatre, Los
    Angeles
Hurlyburly by David Rabe. Produced by Icarus Productions,
    Frederick M. Zollo, Ivan Bloch, and ERB Productions
Ma Rainey's Black Bottom by August Wilson. Produced by Ivan
    Bloch, Robert Cole, and Frederick M. Zollo

DIRECTOR (PLAY)
Keith Hack, *Strange Interlude*
Terry Hands, *Much Ado About Nothing*
Marshall W. Mason, *As Is*
☆ Gene Saks, *Biloxi Blues*

MUSICAL
☆ *Big River*. Produced by Rocco Landesman, Heidi Landesman,
    Rick Steiner, M. Anthony Fisher, and Dodger Productions
Grind. Produced by Kenneth D. Greenblatt, John J. Pomerantz,

Mary Lea Johnson, Martin Richards, James M. Nederlander, Harold Prince, Michael Frazier, Susan Madden Samson, and Jonathan Farkas

Leader of the Pack. Produced by Elizabeth I. McCann, Nelle Nugent, Francine LeFrak, Clive Davis, John Hart Associates, Inc., Rodger Hess, and Richard Kagan

Quilters. Produced by The Denver Center for the Performing Arts, The John F. Kennedy Center for the Performing Arts, The American National Theatre and Academy, and Brockman Seawell

DIRECTOR (MUSICAL)
Barbara Damashek, *Quilters*
Mitch Leigh, *The King and I*
☆ Des McAnuff, *Big River*
Harold Prince, *Grind*

BOOK (MUSICAL)
☆ *Big River* by William Hauptman
Grind by Fay Kanin
Harrigan 'n Hart by Michael Stewart
Quilters by Molly Newman and Barbara Damashek

SCORE
☆ *Big River.* Roger Miller
Grind. Music by Larry Grossman, and lyrics by Ellen Fitzhugh
Quilters. Barbara Damashek

SCENIC DESIGNER
Clarke Dunham, *Grind*
Ralph Koltai, *Much Ado About Nothing*
☆ Heidi Landesman, *Big River*
Voytek and Michael Levine, *Strange Interlude*

COSTUME DESIGNER
☆ Florence Klotz, *Grind*
Patricia McGourty, *Big River*
Alexander Reid, *Cyrano de Bergerac*
Alexander Reid, *Much Ado About Nothing*

LIGHTING DESIGNER
Terry Hands, *Cyrano de Bergerac*
Terry Hands, *Much Ado About Nothing*
Allen Lee Hughes, *Strange Interlude*
☆ Richard Riddell, *Big River*

CHOREOGRAPHER
Category eliminated

REPRODUCTION (PLAY OR MUSICAL)
Cyrano de Bergerac
☆ *Joe Egg*
Much Ado About Nothing
Strange Interlude

SPECIAL AWARDS
☆ Yul Brynner
☆ Edwin Lester
☆ New York State Council on the Arts
☆ Steppenwolf Theater

1986

ACTOR (PLAY)
Hume Cronyn, *The Petition*
Ed Harris, *Precious Sons*
☆ Judd Hirsch, *I'm Not Rappaport*
Jack Lemmon, *Long Day's Journey Into Night*

ACTRESS (PLAY)
Rosemary Harris, *Hay Fever*
Mary Beth Hurt, *Benefactors*
Jessica Tandy, *The Petition*
☆ Lily Tomlin, *The Search for Signs of Intelligent Life in the Universe*

ACTOR (FEATURED ROLE—PLAY)
Peter Gallagher, *Long Day's Journey Into Night*
Charles Keating, *Loot*
Joseph Maher, *Loot*
☆ John Mahoney, *The House of Blue Leaves*

ACTRESS (FEATURED ROLE—PLAY)
Stockard Channing, *The House of Blue Leaves*
☆ Swoosie Kurtz, *The House of Blue Leaves*
Bethel Leslie, *Long Day's Journey Into Night*
Zoe Wanamaker, *Loot*

ACTOR (MUSICAL)
Don Correia, *Singin' in the Rain*
Cleavant Derricks, *Big Deal*
Maurice Hines, *Uptown . . . It's Hot!*
☆ George Rose, *The Mystery of Edwin Drood*

ACTRESS (MUSICAL)
Debbie Allen, *Sweet Charity*
Cleo Laine, *The Mystery of Edwin Drood*
☆ Bernadette Peters, *Song & Dance*
Chita Rivera, *Jerry's Girls*

ACTOR (FEATURED ROLE—MUSICAL)
Christopher d'Ambroise, *Song & Dance*
John Herrera, *The Mystery of Edwin Drood*
Howard McGillin, *The Mystery of Edwin Drood*
☆ Michael Rupert, *Sweet Charity*

ACTRESS (FEATURED ROLE—MUSICAL)
Patti Cohenour, *The Mystery of Edwin Drood*
☆ Bebe Neuwirth, *Sweet Charity*
Jana Schneider, *The Mystery of Edwin Drood*
Elisabeth Welch, *Jerome Kern Goes to Hollywood*

PLAY
Benefactors by Michael Frayn. Produced by James M. Nederlander, Robert Fryer, Douglas Urbanski, Michael Codron, MTM Enterprises, Inc., and CBS Productions
Blood Knot by Athol Fugard. Produced by James B. Freydberg, Max Weitzenhoffer, Lucille Lortel, Estrin Rose Berman Productions, and F.W.M. Producing Group
The House of Blue Leaves by John Guare. Produced by Lincoln Center Theater, Gregory Mosher, and Bernard Gersten
☆ *I'm Not Rappaport* by Herb Gardner. Produced by James Walsh, Lewis Allen, and Martin Heinfling

REPRODUCTION (PLAY OR MUSICAL)
Hay Fever
The Iceman Cometh
Loot
☆ *Sweet Charity*

DIRECTOR (PLAY)
Jonathan Miller, *Long Day's Journey Into Night*
Jose Quintero, *The Iceman Cometh*
John Tillinger, *Loot*
☆ Jerry Zaks, *The House of Blue Leaves*

MUSICAL
Big Deal. Produced by The Shubert Organization, Roger Berlind, Jerome Minskoff, and Jonathan Farkas
☆ *The Mystery of Edwin Drood*. Produced by Joseph Papp

Song & Dance. Produced by Cameron Mackintosh, Inc., The Shubert Organization, F.W.M. Producing Group, and The Really Useful Company, Inc.

Tango Argentino. Produced by Mel Howard and Donald K. Donald

DIRECTOR (MUSICAL)
Bob Fosse, *Big Deal*
☆ Wilford Leach, *The Mystery of Edwin Drood*
Richard Maltby, Jr., *Song & Dance*
Claudio Segovia and Hector Orezzoli, *Tango Argentino*

BOOK (MUSICAL)
Big Deal by Bob Fosse
☆ *The Mystery of Edwin Drood* by Rupert Holmes
Singin' in the Rain by Betty Comden and Adolph Green
Wind in the Willows by Jane Iredale

SCORE
☆ *The Mystery of Edwin Drood*. Rupert Holmes
The News. Paul Schierhorn
Song & Dance. Andrew Lloyd Webber, Don Black, and Richard Maltby, Jr.
Wind in the Willows. William Perry and Roger McGough

SCENIC DESIGNER
Ben Edwards, *The Iceman Cometh*
David Mitchell, *The Boys in Winter*
Beni Montresor, *The Marriage of Figaro*
☆ Tony Walton, *The House of Blue Leaves*

COSTUME DESIGNER
Willa Kim, *Song & Dance*
Beni Montresor, *The Marriage of Figaro*
Ann Roth, *The House of Blue Leaves*
☆ Patricia Zipprodt, *Sweet Charity*

LIGHTING DESIGNER
☆ Pat Collins, *I'm Not Rappaport*
Jules Fisher, *Song & Dance*
Paul Gallo, *The House of Blue Leaves*
Thomas R. Skelton, *The Iceman Cometh*

CHOREOGRAPHER
Graciela Daniele, *The Mystery of Edwin Drood*
☆ Bob Fosse, *Big Deal*
Peter Martins, *Song & Dance*
Tango Argentino Dancers, *Tango Argentino*

SPECIAL AWARD
☆ American Repertory Theater

1987

ACTOR (PLAY)
Philip Bosco, *You Never Can Tell*
☆ James Earl Jones, *Fences*
Richard Kiley, *All My Sons*
Alan Rickman, *Les Liaisons Dangereuses*

ACTRESS (PLAY)
Lindsay Duncan, *Les Liaisons Dangereuses*
☆ Linda Lavin, *Broadway Bound*
Geraldine Page, *Blithe Spirit*
Amanda Plummer, *Pygmalion*

ACTOR (FEATURED ROLE—PLAY)
Frankie R. Faison, *Fences*
☆ John Randolph, *Broadway Bound*
Jamey Sheridan, *All My Sons*
Courtney B. Vance, *Fences*

ACTRESS (FEATURED ROLE—PLAY)
☆ Mary Alice, *Fences*
Annette Bening, *Coastal Disturbances*
Phyllis Newman, *Broadway Bound*
Carole Shelley, *Stepping Out*

ACTOR (MUSICAL)
Roderick Cook, *Oh Coward!*
☆ Robert Lindsay, *Me and My Girl*
Terrence Mann, *Les Misérables*
Colm Wilkinson, *Les Misérables*

ACTRESS (MUSICAL)
Catherine Cox, *Oh Coward!*
☆ Maryann Plunkett, *Me and My Girl*
Teresa Stratas, *Rags*

ACTOR (FEATURED ROLE—MUSICAL)
George S. Irving, *Me and My Girl*
Timothy Jerome, *Me and My Girl*
☆ Michael Maguire, *Les Misérables*
Robert Torti, *Starlight Express*

ACTRESS (FEATURED ROLE—MUSICAL)
Jane Connell, *Me and My Girl*
Judy Kuhn, *Les Misérables*
☆ Frances Ruffelle, *Les Misérables*
Jane Summerhays, *Me and My Girl*

PLAY
Broadway Bound by Neil Simon. Produced by Emanuel Azenberg
Coastal Disturbances by Tina Howe. Produced by Circle in the
    Square, Theodore Mann, and Paul Libin
☆ *Fences* by August Wilson. Produced by Carole Shorenstein
    Hays and The Yale Repertory Theatre
Les Liaisons Dangereuses by Christopher Hampton. Produced by
    James M. Nederlander, The Schubert Organization, Inc.,
    Jerome Minskoff, Elizabeth I. McCann, Stephen Graham, and
    Jonathan Farkas

DIRECTOR (PLAY)
Howard Davies, *Les Liaisons Dangereuses*
Mbongeni Ngema, *Asinamali!*
☆ Lloyd Richards, *Fences*
Carole Rothman, *Coastal Disturbances*

MUSICAL
☆ *Les Misérables*. Produced by Carmeron Mackintosh
Me and My Girl. Produced by Richard Armitage, Terry Allen Kramer,
    James M. Nederlander, Stage Promotions Limited & Co.
Rags. Produced by Lee Guber, Martin Heinfling, Marvin A. Krauss
Starlight Express. Produced by Martin Starger and Lord Grade

DIRECTOR (MUSICAL)
Brian Macdonald, *The Mikado*
☆ Trevor Nunn and ☆ John Caird, *Les Misérables*
Trevor Nunn, *Starlight Express*
Mike Ockrent, *Me and My Girl*

BOOK (MUSICAL)
☆ *Les Misérables* by Alain Boublil and Claude-Michel Schönberg
Me and My Girl by L. Arthur Rose, Douglas Furber, Stephen Fry,
    and Mike Ockrent
Rags by Joseph Stein
Smile by Howard Ashman

SCORE
☆ *Les Misérables*. Music by Claude-Michel Schönberg, lyrics by
    Herbert Kretzmer and Alain Boublil

Me and My Girl. Music by Noel Gay, lyrics by L. Arthur Rose and Douglas Furber

Rags. Music by Charles Strouse, lyrics by Stephen Schwartz

Starlight Express. Music by Andrew Lloyd Webber, lyrics by Richard Stilgoe

Scenic Designer

Bob Crowley, *Les Liaisons Dangereuses*

Martin Johns, *Me and My Girl*

☆ John Napier, *Les Misérables*

Tony Walton, *The Front Page*

Costume Designer

Bob Crowley, *Les Liaisons Dangereuses*

Ann Curtis, *Me and My Girl*

☆ John Napier, *Starlight Express*

Andreane Neofitou, *Les Misérables*

Lighting Designer

Martin Aronstein, *Wild Honey*

☆ David Hersey, *Les Misérables*

David Hersey, *Starlight Express*

Beverly Emmons and Chris Parry, *Les Liaisons Dangereuses*

Choreographer

Ron Field, *Rags*

☆ Gillian Gregory, *Me and My Girl*

Brian Macdonald, *The Mikado*

Arlene Phillips, *Starlight Express*

Best Revival

☆ *All My Sons*. Produced by Jay H. Fuchs, Steven Warnick, and Charles Patsos

The Front Page. Produced by Lincoln Center Theatre, Gregory Mosher, and Bernard Gersten

The Life and Adventures of Nicholas Nickleby. Produced by The Shubert Organization, Three Knights, Ltd., and Robert Fox, Ltd.

Pygmalion. Produced by The Shubert Organization, Jerome Minskoff, and Duncan C. Weldon

Special Awards

☆ George Abbott

☆ Jackie Mason

☆ San Francisco Mime Troupe

1988

ACTOR (PLAY)
Derek Jacobi, *Breaking the Code*
John Lithgow, *M. Butterfly*
Robert Prosky, *A Walk in the Woods*
☆ Ron Silver, *Speed-The-Plow*

ACTRESS (PLAY)
☆ Joan Allen, *Burn This*
Blythe Danner, *A Streetcar Named Desire*
Glenda Jackson, *Macbeth*
Frances McDormand, *A Streetcar Named Desire*

ACTOR (FEATURED ROLE—PLAY)
Michael Gough, *Breaking the Code*
Lou Liberatore, *Burn This*
Delroy Lindo, *Joe Turner's Come and Gone*
☆ B. D. Wong, *M. Butterfly*

ACTRESS (FEATURED ROLE—PLAY)
Kimberleigh Aarn, *Joe Turner's Come and Gone*
☆ L. Scott Caldwell, *Joe Turner's Come and Gone*
Kate Nelligan, *Serious Money*
Kimberly Scott, *Joe Turner's Come and Gone*

ACTOR (MUSICAL)
Scott Bakula, *Romance/Romance*
David Carroll, *Chess*
☆ Michael Crawford, *The Phantom of the Opera*
Howard McGillin, *Anything Goes*

ACTRESS (MUSICAL)
Alison Fraser, *Romance/Romance*
☆ Joanna Gleason, *Into the Woods*
Judy Kuhn, *Chess*
Patti LuPone, *Anything Goes*

ACTOR (FEATURED ROLE—MUSICAL)
Anthony Heald, *Anything Goes*
Werner Klemperer, *Cabaret*
☆ Bill McCutcheon, *Anything Goes*
Robert Westenberg, *Into the Woods*

ACTRESS (FEATURED ROLE—MUSICAL)
☆ Judy Kaye, *The Phantom of the Opera*
Leleti Khumalo, *Sarafina!*

Alyson Reed, *Cabaret*
Regina Resnik, *Cabaret*

PLAY

A *Walk in the Woods* by Lee Blessing. Produced by Lucille Lortel, American Playhouse Theatre Productions, and Yale Repertory Theatre

Joe Turner's Come and Gone by August Wilson. Produced by Elliot Martin, Vy Higginsen, Ken Wydro, and Yale Repertory Theatre

☆ M. *Butterfly* by David Henry Hwang. Produced by Stuart Ostrow and David Geffen

Speed-The-Plow by David Mamet. Produced by Lincoln Center Theater, Gregory Mosher, and Bernard Gersten

DIRECTOR (PLAY)

☆ John Dexter, M. *Butterfly*
Gregory Mosher, *Speed-The-Plow*
Lloyd Richards, *Joe Turner's Come and Gone*
Clifford Williams, *Breaking the Code*

MUSICAL

Into the Woods. Produced by Heidi Landesman, Rocco Landesman, Rick Steiner, M. Anthony Fisher, Frederic H. Mayerson, and Jujamcyn Theatres

☆ *The Phantom of the Opera*. Produced by Cameron Mackintosh and The Really Useful Theatre Company, Inc.

Romance/Romance. Produced by Dasha Epstein, Harve Brosten, Jay S. Bulmash

Sarafina, Produced by Lincoln Center Theater, Gregory Mosher, Bernard Gersten, Lucille Lortel, and The Shubert Organization

DIRECTOR (MUSICAL)

James Lapine, *Into the Woods*
Mbongeni Ngema, *Sarafina!*
☆ Harold Prince, *The Phantom of the Opera*
Jerry Zaks, *Anything Goes*

BOOK (MUSICAL)

The Gospel at Colonus by Lee Breuer
☆ *Into the Woods* by James Lapine
The Phantom of the Opera by Richard Stilgoe and Andrew Lloyd Webber
Romance/Romance by Barry Harman

SCORE (MUSICAL)
☆ *Into the Woods*. Music and lyrics by Stephen Sondheim
The Phantom of the Opera. Music by Andrew Lloyd Webber, lyrics by Charles Hart and Richard Stilgoe
Romance/Romance. Music by Keith Herrmann, lyrics by Barry Harman
Sarafina! Music and lyrics by Mbongeni Ngema and Hugh Masakela

SCENIC DESIGNER
☆ Maria Björnson, *The Phantom of the Opera*
Eiko Ishioka, M. *Butterfly*
Tony Straiges, *Into the Woods*
Tony Walton, *Anything Goes*

COSTUME DESIGNER
☆ Maria Björnson, *The Phantom of the Opera*
Ann Hould-Ward, *Into the Woods*
Eiko Ishioka, M. *Butterfly*
Tony Walton, *Anything Goes*

LIGHTING DESIGNER
☆ Andrew Bridge, *The Phantom of the Opera*
Paul Gallo, *Anything Goes*
Richard Nelson, *Into the Woods*
Andy Phillips, M. *Butterfly*

CHOREOGRAPHER
Lar Lubovitch, *Into the Woods*
Gillian Lynne, *The Phantom of the Opera*
Ndaba Mhlongo and Mbongeni Ngema, *Sarafina!*
☆ Michael Smuin, *Anything Goes*

REVIVAL
☆ *Anything Goes*. Produced by Lincoln Center Theater, Gregory Mosher, and Bernard Gersten
A *Streetcar Named Desire*. Produced by Circle in the Square, Theodore Mann, and Paul Libin
Cabaret. Produced by Barry Weissler and Fran Weissler
Dreamgirls. Produced by Marvin A. Krauss and Irving Siders

SPECIAL AWARDS
☆ Brooklyn Academy of Music
☆ South Coast Repertory of Costa Mesa, CA

1989

Actor (Play)
Mikhail Baryshnikov, *Metamorphosis*
☆ Philip Bosco, *Lend Me A Tenor*
Victor Garber, *Lend Me A Tenor*
Bill Irwin, *Largely New York*

Actress (Play)
Joan Allen, *The Heidi Chronicles*
☆ Pauline Collins, *Shirley Valentine*
Madeline Kahn, *Born Yesterday*
Kate Nelligan, *Spoils of War*

Actor (Featured Role—Play)
Peter Frechette, *Eastern Standard*
☆ Boyd Gaines, *The Heidi Chronicles*
Eric Stoltz, *Our Town*
Gordon Joseph Weiss, *Ghetto*

Actress (Featured Role—Play)
☆ Christine Baranski, *Rumors*
Joanne Camp, *The Heidi Chronicles*
Tovah Feldshuh, *Lend Me A Tenor*
Penelope Ann Miller, *Our Town*

Actor (Musical)
☆ Jason Alexander, *Jerome Robbins' Broadway*
Gabriel Barre, *Starmites*
Brian Lane Green, *Starmites*
Robert La Fosse, *Jerome Robbins' Broadway*

Actress (Musical)
☆ Ruth Brown, *Black and Blue*
Charlotte d'Amboise, *Jerome Robbins' Broadway*
Linda Hopkins, *Black and Blue*
Sharon McNight, *Starmites*

Actor (Featured Role—Musical)
Bunny Briggs, *Black and Blue*
Savion Glover, *Black and Blue*
Scott Wentworth, *Welcome to the Club*
☆ Scott Wise, *Jerome Robbins' Broadway*

Actress (Featured Role—Musical)
Jane Lanier, *Jerome Robbins' Broadway*
Faith Prince, *Jerome Robbins' Broadway*

☆ Debbie Shapiro, *Jerome Robbins' Broadway*
Julie Wilson, *Legs Diamond*

PLAY

Largely New York by Bill Irwin. Produced by James B. Freydberg,
    Kenneth Feld, Jerry L. Cohen, Max Weitzenhoffer, The John F.
    Kennedy Center for the Performing Arts, and The Walt
    Disney Studios
Lend Me A Tenor by Ken Ludwig. Produced by Martin Starger and
    The Really Useful Theatre Co. Inc.
Shirley Valentine by Willy Russell. Produced by The Really Useful
    Theatre Co. Inc. and Bob Swash
☆ *The Heidi Chronicles* by Wendy Wasserstein. Produced by The
    Shubert Organization, Suntory International Corp., James
    Walsh, and Playwrights Horizons

DIRECTOR (PLAY)

Bill Irwin, *Largely New York*
Gregory Mosher, *Our Town*
Daniel Sullivan, *The Heidi Chronicles*
☆ Jerry Zaks, *Lend Me A Tenor*

MUSICAL

Black and Blue. Produced by Mel Howard and Donald K. Donald
☆ *Jerome Robbins' Broadway.* Produced by The Shubert
    Organization, Roger Berlind, Suntory International Corp.,
    Byron Goldman, and Emanuel Azenberg
Starmites. Produced by Hinks Shimberg, Mary Keil, and Steven
    Warnick

DIRECTOR (MUSICAL)

Larry Carpenter, *Starmites*
☆ Jerome Robbins, *Jerome Robbins' Broadway*
Peter Mark Schifter, *Welcome to the Club*
Claudio Segovia and Hector Orezzoli, *Black and Blue*

BOOK (MUSICAL)

Category eliminated for 1989

SCORE (MUSICAL)

Category eliminated for 1989

SCENIC DESIGNER

☆ Santo Loquasto, *Cafe Crown*
Thomas Lynch, *The Heidi Chronicles*
Claudio Segovia and Hector Orezzoli, *Black and Blue*
Tony Walton, *Lend Me A Tenor*

COSTUME DESIGNER
Jane Greenwood, *Our Town*
Willa Kim, *Legs Diamond*
William Ivey Long, *Lend Me A Tenor*
☆ Claudio Segovia and Hector Orezzoli, *Black and Blue*

LIGHTING DESIGNER
Neil Peter Jampolis and Jane Reisman, *Black and Blue*
Brian Nason, *Metamorphosis*
Nancy Schertler, *Largely New York*
☆ Jennifer Tipton, *Jerome Robbins' Broadway*

CHOREOGRAPHER
Michele Assaf, *Starmites*
☆ Cholly Atkins, Henry LeTang, Frankie Manning, and Fayard Nicholas, *Black and Blue*
Bill Irwin, Kimi Okada, *Largely New York*
Alan Johnson, *Legs Diamond*

REVIVAL
Ah, Wilderness! Produced by Ken Marsolais, Alexander H. Cohen, The Kennedy Center for the Performing Arts, Yale Repertory Theatre, Richard Norton, Irma Oestreicher, Elizabeth D. White
Ain't Misbehavin'. Produced by The Shubert Organization, Emanuel Azenberg, Dasha Epstein, and Roger Berlind
Cafe Crown. Produced by LeFrak Entertainment, James M. Nederlander, Francine LeFrak, James L. Nederlander, and Arthur Rubin
☆ *Our Town.* Produced by Lincoln Center Theater, Gregory Mosher, and Bernard Gersten

SPECIAL AWARDS
☆ Hartford Stage Company

The 1990s

"I just remember when I heard Sigourney Weaver announce my name as the winner—it was such a warm sound to my ears . . . as opposed to the three other times I was nominated and I lost, and the sound of another person's name (in that instance) was a harsh sound to my ears.

I was so happy for myself, my wife, who was one of the producers of Jelly's Last Jam, and my family and friends . . . and I was proud to walk up there and receive the Tony® Award for all of us!"

Gregory Hines

"I never dreamed of winning a Tony®—I dreamed of being a part of the American Musical Theatre. So the 'win' for me was the chance to perform a great part in a great musical play. To then be rewarded with 'the prize' was an unexpected, delicious addition to an already amazing personal and professional journey. And the loving reaction from the crowd in the balcony was the best part of a memorable night. In retrospect, the honor is to be included on a list of talented performers that I have so long enjoyed and admired."

Tyne Daly

1990

ACTOR (PLAY)
Charles S. Dutton, *The Piano Lesson*
Dustin Hoffman, *The Merchant of Venice*
Tom Hulce, *A Few Good Men*
☆ Robert Morse, *Tru*

ACTRESS (PLAY)
Geraldine James, *The Merchant of Venice*
Mary-Louise Parker, *Prelude to a Kiss*
☆ Maggie Smith, *Lettice and Lovage*
Kathleen Turner, *Cat on a Hot Tin Roof*

ACTOR (FEATURED ROLE —PLAY)
Rocky Carroll, *The Piano Lesson*
☆ Charles Durning, *Cat on a Hot Tin Roof*
Terry Kinney, *The Grapes of Wrath*
Gary Sinise, *The Grapes of Wrath*

ACTRESS (FEATURED ROLE —PLAY)
Polly Holliday, *Cat on a Hot Tin Roof*
S. Epatha Merkerson, *The Piano Lesson*
Lois Smith, *The Grapes of Wrath*
☆ Margaret Tyzack, *Lettice and Lovage*

ACTOR (MUSICAL)
David Carroll, *Grand Hotel, The Musical*
Gregg Edelman, *City of Angels*
Bob Gunton, *Sweeney Todd*
☆ James Naughton, *City of Angels*

ACTRESS (MUSICAL)
Georgia Brown, *Three Penny Opera*
☆ Tyne Daly, *Gypsy*
Beth Fowler, *Sweeney Todd*
Liliane Montevecchi, *Grand Hotel, The Musical*

ACTOR (FEATURED ROLE —MUSICAL)
René Auberjonois, *City of Angels*
Kevin Colson, *Aspects of Love*
Jonathan Hadary, *Gypsy*
☆ Michael Jeter, *Grand Hotel, The Musical*

ACTRESS (FEATURED ROLE—MUSICAL)
☆ Randy Graff, *City of Angels*
Jane Krakowski, *Grand Hotel, The Musical*

Kathleen Rowe McAllen, *Aspects of Love*
Crista Moore, *Gypsy*

PLAY

Lettice and Lovage by Peter Shaffer. Produced by The Shubert
    Organization, Robert Fox, Ltd., and Roger Berlind
Prelude to a Kiss by Craig Lucas. Produced by Christopher Gould,
    Suzanne Golden, and Dodger Productions
☆ *The Grapes of Wrath* by Frank Galati. Produced by The Shubert
    Organization, Steppenwolf Theatre Company, Suntory
    International Corp., and Jujamcyn Theaters
The Piano Lesson by August Wilson. Produced by Lloyd Richards,
    Yale Repertory Theatre, Center Theatre Group/Ahmanson
    Theatre, Gordon Davidson, Jujamcyn Theaters, Benjamin
    Mordecai, Eugene O'Neill Theatre Center, Huntington
    Theatre Company, Goodman Theatre, and Old Globe Theatre

DIRECTOR (PLAY)

Michael Blakemore, *Lettice and Lovage*
☆ Frank Galati, *The Grapes of Wrath*
Peter Hall, *The Merchant of Venice*
Lloyd Richards, *The Piano Lesson*

MUSICAL

Aspects of Love. Produced by The Really Useful Theatre Company, Inc.
☆ *City of Angels*. Produced by Nick Vanoff, Roger Berlind,
    Jujamcyn Theaters, Suntory International Corp., and The
    Shubert Organization
Grand Hotel, The Musical. Produced by Martin Richards, Mary Lea
    Johnson, Sam Crothers, Sander Jacobs, Kenneth D.
    Greenblatt, Paramount Pictures, Jujamcyn Theaters, Patty
    Grubman, and Marvin A. Krauss
Meet Me in St. Louis. Produced by Brickhill-Burke Productions,
    Christopher Seabrooke, and EPI Products

DIRECTOR (MUSICAL)

Michael Blakemore, *City of Angels*
Trevor Nunn, *Aspects of Love*
Susan H. Schulman, *Sweeney Todd*
☆ Tommy Tune, *Grand Hotel, The Musical*

BOOK (MUSICAL)

Aspects of Love by Andrew Lloyd Webber
☆ *City of Angels* by Larry Gelbart
Grand Hotel, The Musical by Luther Davis
Meet Me in St. Louis by Hugh Wheeler

Score (Musical)

Aspects of Love. Music by Andrew Lloyd Webber, lyrics by Don
   Black, and Charles Hart
☆ *City of Angels.* Music by Cy Coleman, lyrics by David Zippel
Grand Hotel, The Musical. Music and lyrics by Robert Wright,
   George Forrest, and Maury Yeston
Meet Me in St. Louis. Music and lyrics by Hugh Martin and Ralph
   Blane

Scenic Designer

Alexandra Byrne, *Some Americans Abroad*
Kevin Rigdon, *The Grapes of Wrath*
☆ Robin Wagner, *City of Angels*
Tony Walton, *Grand Hotel, The Musical*

Costume Designer

Theoni V. Aldredge, *Gypsy*
Florence Klotz, *City of Angels*
☆ Santo Loquasto, *Grand Hotel, The Musical*
Erin Quigley, *The Grapes of Wrath*

Lighting Designer

☆ Jules Fisher, *Grand Hotel, The Musical*
Paul Gallo, *City of Angels*
Paul Pyant and Neil Peter Jampolis, *Orpheus Descending*
Kevin Rigdon, *The Grapes of Wrath*

Choreographer

Joan Brickhill, *Meet Me in St. Louis*
Graciela Daniele and Tina Paul, *Dangerous Games*
☆ Tommy Tune, *Grand Hotel, The Musical*

Revival

☆ *Gypsy.* Produced by Barry and Fran Weissler, Kathy Levin, and
   Barry Brown
Sweeney Todd. Produced by Circle in the Square Theatre,
   Theodore Mann, and Paul Libin
The Circle. Produced by Elliot Martin, The Shubert Organization,
   and Suntory International Corp.
The Merchant of Venice. Produced by Duncan C. Weldon, Jerome
   Minskoff, Punch Productions, and Peter Hall)

Special Tony® Award

☆ Seattle Repertory Theatre

Tony® Honor

☆ Alfred Drake, For Excellence in the Theatre

1991

ACTOR (PLAY)
Peter Frechette, *Our Country's Good*
☆ Nigel Hawthorne, *Shadowlands*
Tom McGowan, *La Bête*
Courtney B. Vance, *Six Degrees of Separation*

ACTRESS (PLAY)
Stockard Channing, *Six Degrees of Separation*
Julie Harris, *Lucifer's Child*
Cherry Jones, *Our Country's Good*
☆ Mercedes Ruehl, *Lost in Yonkers*

ACTOR (FEATURED ROLE—PLAY)
Adam Arkin, *I Hate Hamlet*
Dylan Baker, *La Bête*
Stephen Lang, *The Speed of Darkness*
☆ Kevin Spacey, *Lost in Yonkers*

ACTRESS (FEATURED ROLE—PLAY)
Amelia Campbell, *Our Country's Good*
Kathryn Erbe, *The Speed of Darkness*
J. Smith-Cameron, *Our Country's Good*
☆ Irene Worth, *Lost in Yonkers*

ACTOR (MUSICAL)
Keith Carradine, *The Will Rogers Follies*
Paul Hipp, *Buddy*
☆ Jonathan Pryce, *Miss Saigon*
Topol, *Fiddler on the Roof*

ACTRESS (MUSICAL)
June Angela, *Shogun: The Musical*
Dee Hoty, *The Will Rogers Follies*
Cathy Rigby, *Peter Pan*
☆ Lea Salonga, *Miss Saigon*

ACTOR (FEATURED ROLE—MUSICAL)
Bruce Adler, *Those Were the Days*
☆ Hinton Battle, *Miss Saigon*
Gregg Burge, *Oh Kay!*
Willy Falk, *Miss Saigon*

ACTRESS (FEATURED ROLE—MUSICAL)
☆ Daisy Eagan, *The Secret Garden*
Alison Fraser, *The Secret Garden*

Cady Huffman, *The Will Rogers Follies*
La Chanze, *Once on This Island*

PLAY

☆ *Lost in Yonkers* by Neil Simon. Produced by Emanuel Azenberg
Our Country's Good by Timberlake Wertenbaker. Produced by
    Frank and Woji Gero, Karl Sydow, Raymond L.Gaspard,
    Frederick Zollo, Diana Bliss, and Hartford Stage Company
Shadowlands by Wiliam Nicholson. Produced by Elliot Martin,
    James M. Nederlander, Brian Eastman, Terry Allen Kramer,
    and Roger L. Stevens
Six Degrees of Seperation by John Guare. Produced by Lincoln
    Center Theatre, Gregory Mosher, and Bernard Gersten

DIRECTOR (PLAY)

Richard Jones, *La Bête*
Mark Lamos, *Our Country's Good*
Gene Saks, *Lost in Yonkers*
☆ Jerry Zaks, *Six Degrees of Separation*

MUSICAL

Miss Saigon. Produced by Cameron Mackintosh
Once on This Island. Produced by The Shubert Organization,
    Capital Cities/ABC Inc., Suntory International, James Walsh,
    and Playwrights Horizons
The Secret Garden. Produced by Heidi Landesman, Rick Steiner,
    Frederic H. Mayerson, Elizabeth Williams, Jujamcyn Theatres,
    TV ASAHI, and Dodger Productions
☆ *The Will Rogers Follies.* Produced by Pierre Cossette, Martin
    Richards, Sam Crothers, James M. Nederlander, Stewart F.
    Lane, Max Weitzenhoffer, and Japan Satellite Broadcasting, Inc.

DIRECTOR (MUSICAL)

Graciela Daniele, *Once on This Island*
Nicholas Hytner, *Miss Saigon*
Eleanor Reissa, *Those Were the Days*
☆ Tommy Tune, *The Will Rogers Follies*

BOOK (MUSICAL)

Miss Saigon by Alain Boubill and Claude-Michel Schönberg
Once on This Island by Lynn Ahrens
☆ *The Secret Garden* by Marsha Norman
The Will Rogers Follies by Peter Stone

SCORE (MUSICAL)

Miss Saigon, Music by Claude-Michel Schönberg, lyrics by Richard
    Maltby, Jr. and Alain Boublil

Once on This Island. Music by Stephen Flaherty, lyrics by Lynn Ahrens
The Secret Garden. Music by Lucy Simon, Lyrics by Marsha Norman
☆ *The Will Rogers Follies.* Music by Cy Coleman, lyrics by Betty Comden and Adolph Green

SCENIC DESIGNER
Richard Hudson, *La Bête*
☆ Heidi Landesman, *The Secret Garden*
John Napier, *Miss Saigon*
Tony Walton, *The Will Rogers Follies*

COSTUME DESIGNER
Theoni V. Aldredge, *The Secret Garden*
Judy Dearing, *Once on This Island*
☆ Willa Kim, *The Will Rogers Follies*
Patricia Zipprodt, *Shogun: The Musical*

LIGHTING DESIGNER
☆ Jules Fisher, *The Will Rogers Follies*
David Hersey, *Miss Saigon*
Allen Lee Hughes, *Once on This Island*
Jennifer Tipton, *La Bête*

CHOREOGRAPHER
Bob Avian, *Miss Saigon*
Graciela Daniele, *Once on This Island*
Dan Siretta, *Oh Kay!*
☆ Tommy Tune, *The Will Rogers Follies*

REVIVAL
☆ *Fiddler on the Roof.* Produced by Barry and Fran Weissler, and Pace Theatrical Group
The Miser. Produced by Circle in the Square Theatre, Theodore Mann, and Paul Libin
Peter Pan. Produced by James M. Nederlander, Arthur Rubin, Thomas P. McCoy, Keith Stava, P.P. Investments, Inc. and Jon B. Platt

SPECIAL TONY® AWARD
☆ Yale Repertory Theater

TONY® HONOR
☆ Father George Moore (given posthumously)

1992

ACTOR (PLAY)
Alan Alda, *Jake's Women*
Alec Baldwin, A *Streetcar Named Desire*
Brian Bedford, *Two Shakespearean Actors*
☆ Judd Hirsch, *Conversations With My Father*

ACTRESS (PLAY)
Jane Alexander, *The Visit*
Stockard Channing, *Four Baboons Adoring The Sun*
☆ Glenn Close, *Death And The Maiden*
Judith Ivey, *Park Your Car in Harvard Yard*

ACTOR (FEATURED ROLE—PLAY)
Roscoe Lee Browne, *Two Trains Running*
☆ Larry Fishburne, *Two Trains Running*
Zeljko Ivanek, *Two Shakespearean Actors*
Tony Shalhoub, *Conversations With My Father*

ACTRESS (FEATURED ROLE—PLAY)
☆ Brid Brennan, *Dancing At Lughnasa*
Rosaleen Linehan, *Dancing At Lughnasa*
Cynthia Martells, *Two Trains Running*
Dearbhla Molloy, *Dancing At Lughnasa*

ACTOR (MUSICAL)
Harry Groener, *Crazy For You*
☆ Gregory Hines, *Jelly's Last Jam*
Nathan Lane, *Guys And Dolls*
Michael Rupert, *Falsettos*

ACTRESS (MUSICAL)
Jodi Benson, *Crazy For You*
Josie de Guzman, *Guys And Dolls*
Sophie Hayden, *The Most Happy Fella*
☆ Faith Prince, *Guys And Dolls*

ACTOR (FEATURED ROLE—MUSICAL)
Bruce Adler, *Crazy For You*
Keith David, *Jelly's Last Jam*
Jonathan Kaplan, *Falsettos*
☆ Scott Waara, *The Most Happy Fella*

ACTRESS (FEATURED ROLE—MUSICAL)
Liz Larsen, *The Most Happy Fella*
☆ Tonya Pinkins, *Jelly's Last Jam*

Vivian Reed, *The High Rollers Social & Pleasure Club*
Barbara Walsh, *Falsettos*

PLAY

☆ *Dancing At Lughnasa* by Brian Friel. Produced by Noel Pearson, Bill Kenwright, and Joseph Harris

Four Baboons Adoring The Sun by John Guare. Produced by Lincoln Center Theater, Andre Bishop, and Bernard Gersten

Two Shakespearean Actors by Richard Nelson. Produced by Lincoln Center Theater, Gregory Mosher, and Bernard Gersten

Two Trains Running by August Wilson. Produced by Yale Repertory Theatre, Stan Wojewodski, Jr., Center Theatre Group/Ahmanson Theatre, Gordon Davidson, Jujamcyn Theaters, Benjamin Mordecai, Huntington Theatre Company, Seattle Repertory Theatre, and Old Globe Theatre

DIRECTOR (PLAY)

Peter Hall, *Four Baboons Adoring The Sun*
☆ Patrick Mason, *Dancing At Lughnasa*
Jack O'Brien, *Two Shakespearean Actors*
Daniel Sullivan, *Conversations With My Father*

MUSICAL

☆ *Crazy For You*. Produced by Roger Horchow and Elizabeth Williams
Falsettos. Produced by Barry and Fran Weissler
Five Guys Named Moe. Produced by Cameron Mackintosh
Jelly's Last Jam. Produced by Margo Lion, Pamela Koslow, Poly-Gram Diversified Entertainment, 126 Second Avenue Corp./Hal Luftig, Roger Hess, Jujamcyn Theaters/TV Asahi, and Herb Alpert

DIRECTOR (MUSICAL)

James Lapine, *Falsettos*
Mike Ockrent, *Crazy For You*
George C. Wolfe, *Jelly's Last Jam*
☆ Jerry Zaks, *Guys And Dolls*

BOOK (MUSICAL)

Crazy For You by Ken Ludwig
☆ *Falsettos* by William Finn and James Lapine
Five Guys Named Moe by Clarke Peters
Jelly's Last Jam by George C. Wolfe

SCORE (MUSICAL)

☆ *Falsettos*. Music and lyrics by William Finn
Jelly's Last Jam. Music by Jelly Roll Morton and Luther Henderson, lyrics by Susan Birkenhead

Metro. Music by Janusz Stoklosa, lyrics by Agata and Maryna Miklaszewska, and Mary Bracken Philips

Nick & Nora. Music by Charles Strouse, lyrics by Richard Maltby, Jr.

Scenic Designer
John Lee Beatty, *A Small Family Business*
Joe Vanek, *Dancing At Lughnasa*
Robin Wagner, *Jelly's Last Jam*
☆ Tony Walton, *Guys And Dolls*

Costume Designer
Jane Greenwood, *Two Shakespearean Actors*
Toni-Leslie James, *Jelly's Last Jam*
☆ William Ivey Long, *Crazy For You*
Joe Vanek, *Dancing At Lughnasa*

Lighting Designer
☆ Jules Fisher, *Jelly's Last Jam*
Paul Gallo, *Crazy For You*
Paul Gallo, *Guys And Dolls*
Richard Pilbrow, *Four Baboons Adoring The Sun*

Choreographer
Terry John Bates, *Dancing At Lughnasa*
Christopher Chadman, *Guys And Dolls*
Hope Clarke, Ted L. Levy, and Gregory Hines, *Jelly's Last Jam*
☆ Susan Stroman, *Crazy For You*

Revival
☆ *Guys And Dolls*. Produced by Dodger Productions, Roger Berlind, Jujamcyn Theaters/TV Asahi, Kardana Productions, and The John F. Kennedy Center for the Performing Arts

The Most Happy Fella. Produced by The Goodspeed Opera House, Center Theatre Group/Ahmanson Theatre, Lincoln Center Theater, The Shubert Organization, and Japan Satellite Broadcasting/Stagevision

On Borrowed Time. Produced by Circle in the Square Theatre, Theodore Mann, Robert Buckley, and Paul Libin

The Visit. Produced by Roundabout Theatre Company, Todd Haimes, and Gene Feist

Special Tony® Award
☆ The Goodman Theatre of Chicago

Tony® Honor
☆ *The Fantasticks*

1993

ACTOR (PLAY)
K. Todd Freeman, *The Song of Jacob Zulu*
☆ Ron Leibman, *Angels in America: Millennium Approaches*
Liam Neeson, *Anna Christie*
Stephen Rea, *Someone Who'll Watch Over Me*

ACTRESS (PLAY)
Jane Alexander, *The Sisters Rosensweig*
☆ Madeline Kahn, *The Sisters Rosensweig*
Lynn Redgrave, *Shakespeare For My Father*
Natasha Richardson, *Anna Christie*

ACTOR (FEATURED ROLE—PLAY)
Robert Sean Leonard, *Candida*
Joe Mantello, *Angels in America: Millennium Approaches*
Zakes Mokae, *The Song of Jacob Zulu*
☆ Stephen Spinella, *Angels in America: Millenium Approaches*

ACTRESS (FEATURED ROLE—PLAY)
Kathleen Chalfant, *Angels in America: Millennium Approaches*
Marcia Gay Harden, *Angels in America: Millennium Approaches*
Anne Meara, *Anna Christie*
☆ Debra Monk, *Redwood Curtain*

ACTOR (MUSICAL)
☆ Brent Carver, *Kiss of the Spider Woman—The Musical*
Tim Curry, *My Favorite Year*
Con O'Neill, *Blood Brothers*
Martin Short, *The Goodbye Girl*

ACTRESS (MUSICAL)
Ann Crumb, *Anna Karenina*
Stephanie Lawrence, *Blood Brothers*
Bernadette Peters, *The Goodbye Girl*
☆ Chita Rivera, *Kiss of the Spider Woman—The Musical*

ACTOR (FEATURED ROLE—MUSICAL)
Michael Cerveris, *The Who's Tommy*
☆ Anthony Crivello, *Kiss of the Spider Woman—The Musical*
Gregg Edelman, *Anna Karenina*
Paul Kandel, *The Who's Tommy*

ACTRESS (FEATURED ROLE—MUSICAL)
Jan Graveson, *Blood Brothers*
Lainie Kazan, *My Favorite Year*

☆ Andrea Martin, *My Favorite Year*
Marcia Mitzman, *The Who's Tommy*

PLAY

☆ *Angels in America: Millennium Approaches* by Tony Kushner.
    Produced by Jujamcyn Theatres, Mark Taper Forum/Gordon
    Davidson, Margo Lion, Susan Quint Gallin, Jon B. Platt, The
    Baruch-Frankel-Viertel Group, Frederick Zollo, and Herb
    Alpert
The Sisters Rosensweig by Wendy Wasserstein. Produced by Lincoln
    Center Theatre, André Bishop, and Bernard Gersten
Someone Who'll Watch Over Me by Frank McGuinness. Produced by
    Noel Pearson, The Shubert Organization, and Joseph Harris
The Song of Jacob Zulu by Tug Yourgrau. Produced by Steppenwolf
    Theatre Company, Randall Arney, Stephen Eich, Albert
    Poland, Susan Liederman, Bette Cerf Hill, and Maurice
    Rosenfield

DIRECTOR (PLAY)

David Leveaux, *Anna Christie*
Eric Simonson, *The Song of Jacob Zulu*
Daniel Sullivan, *The Sisters Rosensweig*
☆ George C. Wolfe, *Angels in America: Millennium Approaches*

MUSICAL

Blood Brothers. Produced by Bill Kenwright
The Goodbye Girl. Produced by Office Two-One Inc., Gladys
    Nederlander, Stewart F. Lane, James M. Nederlander,
    Richard Kagan, and Emanuel Azenberg
☆ *Kiss of the Spider Woman—The Musical*. Produced by The Live
    Entertainment Corp. of Canada/Garth Drabinsky
The Who's Tommy. Produced by PACE Theatrical Group, Dodger
    Productions, and Kardana Productions, Inc.

DIRECTOR (MUSICAL)

Bill Kenwright and Bob Thomson, *Blood Brothers*
Michael Kidd, *The Goodbye Girl*
☆ Des McAnuff, *The Who's Tommy*
Harold Prince, *Kiss of the Spider Woman—The Musical*

BOOK (MUSICAL)

Anna Karenina by Peter Kellogg
Blood Brothers by Willy Russell
☆ *Kiss of the Spider Woman—The Musical* by Terrence McNally
The Who's Tommy by Pete Townshend and Des McAnuff

SCORE (MUSICAL)

Anna Karenina. Music by Daniel Levine, lyrics by Peter Kellogg
☆ *Kiss of the Spider Woman—The Musical*. Music by John Kander, lyrics by Fred Ebb
The Song of Jacob Zulu. Music by Ladysmith Black Mambazo, lyrics by Tug Yourgrau and Ladysmith Black Mambazo
☆ *The Who's Tommy*. Music and lyrics by Pete Townshend

SCENIC DESIGNER

☆ John Arnone, *The Who's Tommy*
John Lee Beatty, *Redwood Curtain*
Jerome Sirlin, *Kiss of the Spider Woman—The Musical*
Robin Wagner, *Angels in America: Millennium Approaches*

COSTUME DESIGNER

Jane Greenwood, *The Sisters Rosensweig*
☆ Florence Klotz, *Kiss of the Spider Woman—The Musical*
Erin Quigley, *The Song of Jacob Zulu*
David C. Woolard, *The Who's Tommy*

LIGHTING DESIGNER

Howell Binkley, *Kiss of the Spider Woman—The Musical*
Jules Fisher, *Angels in America: Millennium Approaches*
Dennis Parichy, *Redwood Curtain*
☆ Chris Parry, *The Who's Tommy*

CHOREOGRAPHER

☆ Wayne Cilento, *The Who's Tommy*
Graciela Daniele, *The Goodbye Girl*
Vincent Paterson and Rob Marshall, *Kiss of the Spider Woman—The Musical*
Randy Skinner, *Ain't Broadway Grand*

REVIVAL

☆ *Anna Christie*. Produced by Roundabout Theatre Company and Todd Haimes
Saint Joan. Produced by National Actors Theatre, Tony Randall, and Duncan C. Weldon
The Price. Produced by Roundabout Theatre Company and Todd Haimes
Wilder, Wilder, Wilder. Produced by Circle in the Square Theatre, Theodore Mann, George Elmer, Paul Libin, Willow Cabin Theatre Company, Edward Berkeley, Adam Oliensis, and Maria Radman

Special Tony® Awards
☆ Oklahoma! —50th Anniversary
☆ La Jolla Playhouse

Tony® Honors
☆ IATSE
☆ Broadway Cares/Equity Fights AIDS

1994

Actor (Play)
Brian Bedford, *Timon of Athens*
Christopher Plummer, *No Man's Land*
☆ Stephen Spinella, *Angels in America: Perestroika*
Sam Waterston, *Abe Lincoln in Illinois*

Actress (Play)
Nancy Marchand, *Black Comedy*
☆ Diana Rigg, *Medea*
Joan Rivers, *Sally Marr . . . and Her Escorts*
Anna Deavere Smith, *Twilight: Los Angeles, 1992*

Actor (Featured Role—Play)
Larry Bryggman, *Picnic*
David Marshall Grant, *Angels in America: Perestroika*
Gary Itzin, *The Kentucky Cycle*
☆ Jeffrey Wright, *Angels in America: Perestroika*

Actress (Featured Role—Play)
☆ Jane Adams, *An Inspector Calls*
Debra Monk, *Picnic*
Jeanne Paulsen, *The Kentucky Cycle*
Anne Pitoniak, *Picnic*

Actor (Musical)
☆ Boyd Gaines, *She Loves Me*
Victor Garber, *Damn Yankees*
Terrence Mann, *Beauty and the Beast*
Jere Shea, *Passion*

Actress (Musical)
Susan Egan, *Beauty and the Beast*
Dee Hoty, *The Best Little Whorehouse Goes Public*
Judy Kuhn, *She Loves Me*
☆ Donna Murphy, *Passion*

ACTOR (FEATURED ROLE—MUSICAL)
Tom Aldredge, *Passion*
Gary Beach, *Beauty and the Beast*
☆ Jarrod Emick, *Damn Yankees*
Jonathan Freeman, *She Loves Me*

ACTRESS (FEATURED ROLE—MUSICAL)
Marcia Lewis, *Grease*
Sally Mayes, *She Loves Me*
Marin Mazzie, *Passion*
☆ Audra Ann McDonald, *Carousel*

PLAY
☆ *Angels in America: Perestroika* by Tony Kushner. Produced by Jujamcyn Theatres and The Mark Taper Forum/Gordon Davidson, Artistic Director with Margo Lion, Susan Quint Gallin, John B. Platt, The Baruch-Frankel-Viertel Group, and Frederick Zollo in association with the New York Shakespeare Festival, Mordecai/Cole Productions, and Herb Alpert.
Broken Glass by Arthur Miller. Produced by Robert Whitehead/Roger L. Stevens/Lars Schmidt, Spring Sirkin, and Terry and Timothy Childs.
The Kentucky Cycle by Robert Schenkkan. Produced by David Richenthal, Gene R. Korf, Roger L. Stevens, Jennifer Manocherian, Annette Niemtzow, Mark Taper Forum/Intiman Theatre Company, The John F. Kennedy Center for the Performing Arts in association with Benjamin Mordecai.
Twilight: Los Angeles, 1992 by Anna Deavere Smith. Produced by Benjamin Mordecai, Laura Rafaty, Ric Wanetik, The New York Shakespeare Festival, and Mark Taper Forum.

DIRECTOR (PLAY)
☆ Stephen Daldry, *An Inspector Calls*
Gerald Gutierrez, *Abe Lincoln in Illinois*
Michael Langham, *Timon of Athens*
George C. Wolfe, *Angels in America: Perestroika*

MUSICAL
A Grand Night for Singing. Produced by Roundabout Theatre Company, Todd Haimes, Artistic Director.
Beauty and the Beast. Produced by Walt Disney Theatrical Productions/Robert McTyre and Ron Logan.
Cyrano: The Musical. Produced by Joop van den Ende in association with Peter T. Kulok.

☆ *Passion*. Produced by The Shubert Organization, Capital Cities/ABC, Roger Berlind, and Scott Rudin.

DIRECTOR (MUSICAL)
Scott Ellis, *She Loves Me*
☆ Nicholas Hytner, *Carousel*
James Lapine, *Passion*
Robert Jess Roth, *Beauty and the Beast*

BOOK (MUSICAL)
A Grand Night for Singing by Walter Bobbie
Beauty and the Beast by Linda Woolverton
Cyrano: The Musical by Koen Van Kijk
☆ *Passion* by James Lapine

ORIGINAL MUSICAL SCORE
Beauty and the Beast. Music by Alan Menken, lyrics by Howard Ashman and Tim Rice.
Cyrano: The Musical. Music by Ad van Dijk, lyrics by Koen van Dijk, Peter Reeves, and Sheldon Harnick.
☆ *Passion*. Music and lyrics by Stephen Sondheim.

SCENIC DESIGNER
☆ Bob Crowley, *Carousel*
Peter J. Davison, *Medea*
Ian MacNeil, *An Inspector Calls*
Tony Walton, *She Loves Me*

COSTUME DESIGNER
David Charles and Jane Greenwood, *She Loves Me*
Jane Greenwood, *Passion*
☆ Ann Hould-Ward, *Beauty and the Beast*
Yan Tax, *Cyrano: The Musical*

LIGHTING DESIGNER
Beverly Emmons, *Passion*
Jules Fisher, *Angels in America: Perestroika*
☆ Rick Fisher, *An Inspector Calls*
Natasha Katz, *Beauty and the Beast*

CHOREOGRAPHER
Jeff Calhoun, *Grease*
☆ Sir Kenneth MacMillan, *Carousel*
Rob Marshall, *Damn Yankees*
Rob Marshall, *She Loves Me*

REVIVAL

Abe Lincoln in Illinois. Produced by Lincoln Center Theatre, Andre Bishop, and Bernard Gersten.

☆ *An Inspector Calls*. Produced by Noel Pearson, The Shubert Organization, Capital Cities/ABC, and Joseph Harris.

Medea. Produced by Bill Kenwright.

Timon of Athens. Produced by National Actors Theatre and Tony Randall.

REVIVAL (MUSICAL)

☆ *Carousel*. Produced by Lincoln Center Theatre, Andre Bishop, Bernard Gersten, The Royal National Theatre, Cameron Mackintosh, and The Rodgers & Hammerstein Organization.

Damn Yankees. Produced by Mitchell Maxwell, PolyGram Diversified Entertainment, Dan Markley, Kevin McCollum, Victoria Maxwell, Fred H. Krones, Andrea Nasher, The Frankel-Viertel-Baruch Group, Paula Heil Fisher, Julie Ross, Jon B. Platt, Alan Schuster, and Peter Breger.

Grease. Produced by Barry and Fran Weissler and Jujamcyn Theatres.

She Loves Me. Produced by Roundabout Theatre Company, Todd Haimes, James M. Nederlander, Elliott Martin, Herbert Wasserman, Freddy Beinstock, and Roger L. Stevens.

SPECIAL TONY® AWARDS

Jessica Tandy and Hume Cronyn: Lifetime Achievement
McCarter Theatre: Regional Theatre

Rules and Regulations of the American Theatre Wing's Tony® Awards 1993–94 Season

The following are the Tony Awards Rules and Regulations for the 1993–94 theatrical season and are subject to change without notice:

1. ADMINISTRATION

(a) The Antoinette Perry (Tony) Awards Administration Committee (*"Tony Awards Administration Committee"*) shall administer the American Theatre Wing's Tony Awards, pursuant to the rules of governance established by the Tony Management Committee from time to time. The following provisions of this paragraph 1(a) set forth the current rules of governance:

The Tony Awards Administration Committee shall be a self-governing body comprised of 24 members, 10 of whom shall be designees of the American Theatre Wing (*"Wing"*), 10 of whom shall be designees of The League of American Theatres and Producers (*"League"*) and one member each from The Dramatists Guild, Inc.,

Actors' Equity Association, United Scenic Artists and Society of Stage Directors and Choreographers. The Tony Awards Administration Committee shall meet from time to time and, among other duties, shall have the responsibility of determining eligibility for nominations in all award categories. Except as provided in paragraph 1(b) herein, in order to take any action there must be a quorum consisting of 16 members of the Tony Awards Administration Committee. In order to be eligible for nomination, a potential candidate for nomination must receive an affirmative vote of a majority of those members present. Any other action (other than changes in these Rules and Regulations) shall require the affirmative vote of two-thirds of those members present. Changes in these Rules and Regulations shall require 16 votes; *provided, however*, that only the Tony Management Committee may make changes in the provisions of this paragraph 1(a). Proxies are not permitted in any vote of the Tony Awards Administration Committee; however, in order to provide continuity, the Wing and the League shall each appoint up to 5 alternate designees and each of the other organizations represented on the Tony Awards Administration Committee shall each appoint one alternate designee. Each of the alternate designees shall have the right to attend Tony Awards Administration Committee meetings, but shall not have the right to vote at such meetings unless such alternate designee's principal designee is unable to attend, in which case the vote of such alternate shall be valid and binding as if made by the alternate's principal. All decisions of the Tony Awards Administration Committee concerning eligibility for the Awards and all other matters relating to their administration and presentation, including adoption of amendments to these Rules and Regulations, shall be final.

(b) Notwithstanding the foregoing requirement that 16 members of the Tony Awards Administration Committee are needed to constitute a quorum, the Tony Awards Administration Committee may permit a subcommittee, consisting of 10 members, to convene on the day of nominations in order to answer any question which the Nominating Committee may have and to take any action which may be necessary (other than changes in these Rules and Regulations or actions in direct contravention of any action previously taken by the full Administration Committee). The 10 members of the subcommittee shall consist of 4 members to be chosen by the League from its designees on the Tony Awards Administration Committee, 4 by the Wing from its designees and 2 by agreement among The Dramatists Guild, Inc., Actors' Equity Association, the United Scenic Artists and the Society of Stage

Directors and Choreographers from among their combined designees. In order to answer any question posed by the Nominating Committee or to take any permitted action, there must be a quorum consisting of 7 members of such subcommittee and an affirmative vote of two-thirds of those members present, except in cases regarding questions of eligibility of a potential candidate for nomination, which shall require an affirmative vote of a majority of those members present.

2. ELIGIBILITY FOR NOMINATION

(a) In order for the Tony Awards Administration Committee to determine that a production is eligible in the various categories for nomination for a Tony Award, all of the following six requirements must be satisfied:

(i) the production must be, in the judgment of the Tony Awards Administration Committee, a legitimate theatrical production

(ii) which "officially opens" (as defined in paragraph 2(e) herein)

(iii) in an "eligible Broadway theatre" (as set forth on Exhibit A)

(iv) on or before the "Eligibility Date" of the current season (as defined in paragraph 2(e) herein)

(v) and the producer of the production must invite, in a timely manner and free of charge, each of the eligible Tony voters to attend a performance of the production. Invitations shall be extended, in a manner prescribed by the Tony Administration Committee, on or before the Eligibility Date of the current season. For this purpose, the producer must make available at least 8 "paid performances" of the production (i.e. previews, opening and/or regular performances in an eligible Broadway theatre) which are presented on or before the Monday prior to the presentation of the Awards. This requirement shall be subject to the following exception: If a production which officially opens in an eligible Broadway theatre on or before the Eligibility Date is unable to satisfy the 8 paid performance requirement because it closes prior to presenting 8 paid performances, the production may nevertheless be deemed eligible *provided that* the producer has invited and made tickets available to the Tony voters for at least one-half of all paid performances presented in an eligible Broadway theatre prior to the closing

(vi) and the producer must certify in writing to the Tony Awards Administration Committee that the producer has fully complied with the Rules and Regulations of the Tony Awards Administration Committee regarding the invitation of Tony voters. Such certification must be received prior to the Eligibility Date.

(b) In order for the production to be eligible in the various categories, any play or musical which was previously presented professionally in the Borough of Manhattan (other than as a show-case, workshop or so-called "letter of agreement" production) in a non-eligible theatre must transfer to an eligible theatre no later than 30 weeks from its official opening in the non-eligible theatre. If the production transfers after the Eligibility Date of the current theatrical season, but within the 30-week period, such production shall be eligible in the various categories for the following theatrical season.

(c) In order for the production to be eligible in the Best Play or Best Musical category, a play or musical may contain elements which substantially duplicate elements of productions previously presented professionally in the Borough of Manhattan (other than as showcase, workshop or so-called "letter of agreement" productions) only if, in the judgment of the Tony Administration Committee, those duplicated elements in their totality create a new play or musical.

(d) *Ineligibility of Production/Eligibility of Elements.* If the production meets the requirements of paragraphs 2(a)(i) through (vi) and 2(b) herein, but fails to satisfy any of the requirements set forth in paragraph 2(c), the production shall automatically be ineligible to receive a nomination in the Best Play, or Best Musical categories; however, such failure shall not adversely affect the eligibility of any of the individual elements (i.e. playwrights, bookwriters, composers, lyricists, actors, designers, directors and choreographers) who are otherwise eligible to receive nominations or awards in their respective categories.

(e) *Definitions.* For the purposes of these Rules and Regulations, the term *"official opening"* shall mean the performance of the production which the producer has publicly announced as being the official opening; the term *"Eligibility Date"* shall mean the date which the Tony Awards Administration Committee establishes as the cut-off date for eligibility. The Eligibility Date for the current season shall be at least 32 days prior to the date on which the Awards are to be presented.

(f) *Theatres.* In order to qualify as an eligible Broadway theatre a theatre must have 500 or more seats and be deemed otherwise qualified by the Tony Awards Administration Committee. A list of eligible Broadway theatres is attached hereto as Exhibit A. Qualifying theatres may be added to such list by the Tony Awards Administration Committee at any time prior to February 1 of the .current season. A theatre so added to the list of eligible theatres shall be eligible only from the effective date of its addition.

(g) *Classics.* Plays or musicals which are determined by the Tony Awards Administration Committee to be "classics" shall not be eligible for an Award in the Best Play or Best Musical category but shall be eligible in the Best Revival category provided they meet all other eligibility requirements set forth in these Rules.

(h) *Revivals.* Each year the Tony Awards Administration Committee shall determine whether there shall exist in quality and quantity a sufficient number of Revivals to merit the granting of an Award for Best Revival of a Play or Musical. A "*Revival*" shall be any play or musical presented in an eligible theatre which (A) is a "classic" (as described in paragraph 2(g) herein), or (B) is a play or musical previously presented professionally in substantially the same form in the Borough of Manhattan (other than as a showcase, workshop or so-called "letter of agreement" production) which has not had such a prior professional performance in the Borough of Manhattan during the 3 years immediately preceding the Eligibility Date. In addition, if a production opens in an ineligible theatre (and otherwise meets all of the requirements set forth herein for Revivals) and transfers to an eligible theatre within the time set forth in Paragraph 2(b) herein, such transferred production is eligible as a Revival. The determination that a play or musical is ineligible in the Best Play or Best Musical category by reason of Paragraph 2(c) shall not, by itself, make the play or musical eligible in the Best Revival category unless such play or musical also meets the requirements of this paragraph 2(h). Whether or not a play or musical is eligible for the Best Revival category, the elements of such production shall be eligible in those categories in which said elements do not, in the judgment of the Tony Awards Administration Committee, substantially duplicate the prior production of the play or musical, and provided the Play or Musical otherwise meets all of the requirements set forth herein for Revivals.

(i) *Producers.* Only those producers listed above the title in the opening night program shall be eligible for nomination for a Tony Award. Regardless of the number of eligible producers for a particular production, the number of medallions to be presented shall be limited to 2 for the Award to Producer of the Best Play, 2 for the Award to Producer of the Best Musical, and 2 for the Award to Producer of Best Revival of a Play or Musical.

(j) *Determination of Eligible Candidates for Nomination.* (A) The Tony Awards Administration Committee shall submit to the Nominating Committee (as described in paragraph 5 herein) a list of the eligible candidates for nomination in each Award category. The Tony Awards Administration Committee shall determine whether a sufficient number of eligible candidates exist in quality or quantity to merit the granting of an Award in the applicable category for the current season. The Tony Awards Administration Committee shall also have the sole discretion to reduce the number of nominees to fewer than four, but, in no event, fewer than two in a particular category for the current season. The Nominating Committee may request that the duly-appointed subcommittee, described in paragraph 1(b) herein, make any such reduction. Eligibility for nomination in the Best Performance categories shall be limited to one Actor or Actress for each nomination in such categories.

(B) In determining in which Award category any eligible candidate (person or production) shall be placed, the Tony Awards Administration Committee shall use the opening night program as its initial guide, together with any additional guidelines promulgated by said Committee.

(1)   If a producer of a particular production wishes to propose that an eligible candidate be placed in a category other than that indicated by the opening night program, the producer may send a written request to the Tony Awards Administration Committee setting forth the producer's reasons for asking the Committee to consider such a change. Such request cannot be considered if sent later than two weeks following the official opening of such production.

(2)   No member of the Tony Awards Administration Committee who has an interest of any nature in a particular production may propose, with respect to such production, that an eligible candidate be placed in a category other than that indicated by the opening night program or vote on such a proposed change (regardless of whether a request for such change has been timely made by the producer or by anyone else); however, such interested member may participate in discussions regarding such proposed change. The vote required to pass such a category change shall be a majority of those members present who are not ineligible to vote by reason of this paragraph. A member of the Committee shall not be ineligible to propose or vote on a category change in a particular production if such member's sole interest of any nature in such production is that

member's affiliation with the same union, guild or organization which has as one of its members, a person who has an interest of any nature in such production.

(3)　　Once the placement of an eligible candidate in a category has been decided on by the Tony Awards Administration Committee, the placement cannot be changed at a later date.

3. THE AWARDS PRESENTATION AND ELIGIBILITY DATE

(a) The Awards shall be presented during the theatrical season but not earlier than May 24th of such season, unless the network broadcasting the Awards chooses to do so and gives 4 months notice prior to the date selected for broadcast. The date of the presentation ceremony shall be announced as soon as it has been determined.

(b) The Eligibility Date for nominations shall be announced as soon as it has been determined.

4. CATEGORIES OF AWARDS

(a) The Awards may, subject to the provisions of these Rules and Regulations, be made in the following categories:

> Best Play—Award to Author; Award to Producer
> Best Musical—Award to Producer
> Best Book of a Musical
> Best Original Score (Music & Lyrics) Written for the Theatre
> Best Performance by a leading Actor in a Play
> Best Performance by a leading Actress in a Play
> Best Performance by a leading Actor in a Musical
> Best Performance by a leading Actress in a Musical
> Best Performance by a featured Actor in a Play
> Best Performance by a featured Actress in a Play
> Best Performance by a featured Actor in a Musical
> Best Performance by a featured Actress in a Musical
> Best Direction of a Play
> Best Direction of a Musical
> Best Scenic Design
> Best Costume Design
> Best Lighting Design
> Best Choreography
> Best Revival of a Play or Musical (see paragraph 2(i))

(b) The Tony Awards Administration Committee may, in its discretion, give a "Special Tony Award" to a regional theatre company upon the recommendation of an organization chosen by the Tony Awards Administration Committee (currently the American Theatre Critics Association) which organization shall apply objective and fair standards to determine that such regional theatre company has displayed a continuous level of artistic achievement contributing to the growth of theatre nationally.

(c) The Tony Awards Administration Committee may, in its discretion, give a "Special Tony Award" for lifetime achievement in the theatre.

(d) The Tony Awards Administration Committee may, in its discretion, give a "Special Tony Award" to a theatrical event that "officially opens" in an "eligible Broadway theatre" on or before the "Eligibility Date" of the current season, but which does not fit into any existing Tony Award category, which "Special Tony Award" shall be designated to be awarded to the production or any element thereof.

(e) Only the Tony Award winners for the categories listed in Paragraph 4(a) above and recipients of the Regional Theatre Special Tony Award and other Special Tony Awards shall receive Tony Award medallions.

(f) "Tony Honors for Excellence in the Theatre" may be given in the discretion of the Tony Awards Administration Committee. Such Honors shall be granted only if the Tony Awards Administration Committee, after applying objective and fair standards, determines that the candidate has made contributions qualifying for "excellence in the theatre." Anyone may, not later than 30 days prior to the Eligibility Date, recommend in writing a candidate for Tony Honors consideration by the Tony Awards Administration Committee.

5. SELECTION OF WINNERS OF REGULAR AWARDS
(a) The Nominating Committee.

(i) The "Nominating Committee" shall be appointed by the Tony Awards Administration Committee and shall consist of from 9 to 18 persons. The Nominating Committee shall be selected so as to assure that each eligible production and performer shall have been seen by as many members as possible. Members of the Nominating Committee shall make every effort to attend a preview or opening night performance. Travel expenses shall not be provided to members of the Nominating Committee.

(ii) The Nominating Committee shall meet on the third business day following the Eligibility Date of the current season, or as soon thereafter as possible. At such meeting, the Nominating Committee shall be given a separate ballot for each category containing a list compiled by the Tony Awards Administration Committee of the possible candidates for nomination in said category. The Nominating Committee shall openly discuss the qualifications of the possible candidates for each category. At the conclusion of discussion of each category, each member of the Nominating Committee shall cast his/her secret ballot and such ballot shall be collected by a representative of the independent accounting firm selected pursuant to paragraph 5(f) of these Rules and Regulations. The vote of each member of the Nominating Committee must be based on the ballot and list so submitted. The foregoing procedure shall continue until the voting has been completed in all categories. Neither write-in votes nor proxies shall be permitted. The independent accounting firm shall tabulate the votes of the Nominating Committee and shall announce the nominees to the members of the Nominating Committee and the Tony Administration Committee. The actual number of votes received by those eligible (including the nominees) in each category shall not be disclosed by such accounting firm to anyone on the Tony Awards Administration Committee or to any other person or entity. The Tony Awards Administration Committee (or a subcommittee duly appointed as described in paragraph 1(b) herein) will meet on the day of nominations in order to answer any question which the Nominating Committee may have and to take any action which may be necessary but the subcommittee will not have the authority to take any action in direct contravention of any action previously taken by the full Administration Committee.

(iii)   The voting for nominees shall be on a cumulative (i.e. *"weighted"*) basis. Each category must receive four votes on a weighted basis.* For example, if there are twenty candidates in a category, the vote shall be 4-3-2 or 1 in a descending order of preference of the member of the Nominating Committee. The weight given will depend upon the discretion of the person voting; *provided, however,* that

---

*If there are three or fewer eligible candidates in a category pursuant to paragraph 2(j), the above voting procedure shall be deemed modified accordingly. For example, if only three eligible candidates are suggested in a category, the weighted vote shall be 3-2-1 or "0" in lieu of "1" and the nominations shall be conferred upon those eligible candidates that receive the three highest total votes. If there are only two eligible candidates in a category, no "0" votes may be cast.

each member of the Nominating Committee shall be required to cast all the votes in each category in the manner described above. Once the categories have been established by the Tony Awards Administration Committee, the Nominating Committee shall have no power to eliminate a category. If there are 4 or fewer eligible candidates, each member of the Nominating Committee may cast a "0" vote rather than a "1" vote for any such eligible candidate whom such member deems unworthy of a nomination.*

(b) *The Number of Nominees.* There shall be four nominees in each category (subject to the provisions of paragraph 2(j) herein). The nominations shall be conferred upon those eligible persons or productions in each category that receive the four highest total votes based on the weighted system described above.* In the event the vote of the Nominating Committee results in a tie that would otherwise necessitate more than four nominations in a category, said tie shall be broken in the following manner. The independent accounting firm shall determine which candidate among those tied received the highest number of "4" votes. The candidate with the highest number of "4" votes among those tied shall receive the nomination. If any of those tied have the same number of "4" votes, the independent accounting firm shall then determine which of said candidates received the highest number of "3" votes, in which event the candidate with the highest number of "3" votes shall receive the nomination. Should further ties still result, the independent accounting firm shall continue the process to determine which of the candidates among those tied received the highest number of "2" votes, in which event the nomination shall be conferred upon the candidate with the highest number of "2" votes. If, after following the foregoing procedure, the vote remains tied, the members of the Nominating Committee shall recast their votes until the tie is broken.

(c) *Persons Eligible to Vote.* The persons eligible to vote for the purpose of determining winners of the Tony Awards shall be the members of the governing boards of the following organizations:

1. Actors' Equity Association
2. The Dramatists Guild
3. Society of Stage Directors & Choreographers
4. United Scenic Artists

*See prior footnote.
*See prior footnote.

and those persons whose names appear on the Designated Press Performances and First Night List, the Board of Directors of the American Theatre Wing (not to exceed 45 persons), the Full Members of The League of American Theatres and Producers, Inc. and no more than 8 members of the Theatrical Council of the Casting Society of America who meet the criteria agreed between the Tony Awards Administration Committee and the Casting Society of America. Employees (other than the Executive Director or equivalent) of any of the foregoing organizations shall not be eligible to vote for the winners of the Tony Awards.

The Tony Awards Administration Committee shall have the right, in its discretion, to remove any person from eligibility to vote in the current season in the event said person has not exercised his/her right to vote in the prior season or who violates any rule herein.

(d) *Ballots of Persons Eligible to Vote.* No ballot shall be counted unless the voter casting it has certified to the Tony Awards Administration Committee that, with respect to each category in which the voter has voted, the voter has seen a performance of each production which has been nominated for an Award and a performance by each performer who has been nominated in the production with respect to which such performer has been nominated. The ballot may provide that marking and returning it constitutes such a certification. Write-in votes shall not be permitted.

(e) *Identity of Eligible Voters.* As complete a list as possible of all such eligible voters shall be sent to each producer prior to the first paid public performance of the production.

(f) *Independent Accounting Firm.* An independent accounting firm shall be selected by the Tony Awards Administration Committee, subject to the approval of the television network over which the program is broadcast, if such approval is required pursuant to the terms of the contract with such network. The firm selected shall mail a ballot containing the names of the nominees to each eligible voter at least 14 days prior to the date on which the Awards are to be presented, with a request to mail completed ballots directly to the independent accounting firm. Such firm shall count and tabulate those ballots received by the close of business on Friday prior to the presentation of the Awards and shall certify the winners to the Tony Awards Administration Committee.

(g) *Selection of Winners.* The winner in each category shall be the nominee in that category receiving the highest number of votes. No tabulation of the numbers of votes for each nominee shall be disclosed to the Tony Awards Administration Committee or Nominating Committee or to any other person or entity, and the names of the winners shall not be similarly disclosed until the presentation of the Awards.

6. USE OF TONY AWARDS DESIGNATION IN ADVERTISING

Whenever the Tony Award designation is used in advertising media by or on behalf of a nominee or winner, such use must conform to the following conditions:

(a) *In the Case of a Nominee*:

Such use must specify the category for which the nomination is made as well as the fact that the nominee has received a nomination, not an Award.

To accomplish these objectives, use of the words "Tony® Awards" must immediately precede or follow the words "Nominated for," "Nominee" or "Nomination" in the same size type as the words "Tony® Awards." Use of the word "Winner" shall be prohibited when used in connection with the receipt of a nomination, a Special Tony Award or Tony Honors for Excellence in the Theatre.

Once the Awards have been announced for any given season, the use of the Tony Award designation on behalf of a nominee in any advertising media in the metropolitan New York area shall be discontinued within three months following the date of said announcement.

(b) *In the Case of a Winner*:

Such use must specify the season and the category for which the Award was granted and such specification must immediately precede or follow the words "Tony® Award" in the same size type as the words "Tony® Award."

If, in the sole opinion of the Tony Awards Administration Committee, any of the above provisions have been violated, said violation must be corrected within ten days following the delivery of written notice of such violation. If such violation has not been so corrected within the ten-day time period, the Producer engaging in said violation shall be removed as a Tony voter in the next succeeding year. With respect to any other advertising practice which, in the sole opinion of the Tony Awards Administration Committee, is deceptive to the public, the Tony Awards Administration Committee shall, in addition to removal of the Producer as a Tony voter, take whatever action is necessary to prevent such deceptive practices.

EXHIBIT A

Eligible Theatres

Ambassador 215 West 49 Street	Gershwin 1633 Broadway	Minskoff 200 West 45 Street
Brooks Atkinson 256 West 47 Street	John Golden 252 West 45 Street	Music Box 239 West 45 Street
Ethel Barrymore 243 West 47 Street	*Helen Hayes 240 West 44 Street	Nederlander 208 West 41 Street
Vivian Beaumont 150 West 65 Street	Imperial 249 West 45 Street	Eugene O'Neill 230 West 49 Street
Martin Beck 302 West 45 Street	Walter Kerr 225 West 48 Street	Palace 1564 Broadway
Belasco 111 West 44 Street	Longacre 220 West 48 Street	Plymouth 236 West 45 Street
Booth 222 West 47 Street	Lunt-Fontanne 205 West 46 Street	Richard Rodgers 226 West 46 Street
Broadhurst 235 West 44 Street	Lyceum 149 West 45 Street	Royale 242 West 45 Street
Broadway 1681 Broadway	Majestic 245 West 44 Street	St. James 246 West 44 Street
Circle in the Square 1633 Broadway	Marquis Marriott Hotel 1535 Broadway	Shubert 225 West 44 Street
Cort 138 West 48 Street		Neil Simon 250 West 52 Street
*Criterion Center Stage Right 1530 Broadway		Virginia 245 West 52 Street
		Winter Garden 1634 Broadway

These theatres were deemed "eligible Broadway theatres" prior to the amendment of the rule (effective for the 1989–90 Season) which increased the minimum seating requirement from 499 to 500 and thus, each of the theatres are "grandfathered" and continue to be deemed eligible provided they do not reduce their seating capacity to below the number of seats such theatres made available to the public on June 1, 1989. In the September 19, 1991 Rule revisions, The Edison Theatre was deemed to have become ineligible because of such a reduction in seating capacity.

Index

Page numbers in boldface indicate the location of a Tony® Award winner.

Index

Index

Index

Index

Index